Race

Race

Ryland Fisher

First published by Jacana Media (Pty) Ltd in 2007

10 Orange Street
Sunnyside
Auckland Park 2092
South Africa
+2711 628 3200
www.jacana.co.za

ISBN 978-1-77009-373-7

Set in Sabon 10.5/15 pt
Printed by CTP Book Printers, Cape Town
Job No. 000442

See a complete list of Jacana titles at www.jacana.co.za

I have decided to dedicate this book to my mother and father, who have both passed away. I owe my identity to them and want to thank them for giving me the greatest gift on earth: life. They also gave me enough freedom to ask questions about life and not just to accept things at face value. For that, I will be eternally grateful to them.

CONTENTS

ACKNOWLEDGEMENTS

While one person's name appears as the author of any book, there are normally many people who helped to make it happen. This book is no exception.

I have to thank Sir Anthony O'Reilly, the Chairman of Independent News and Media, for giving me an initial allowance that made it possible for me to take some time off to conduct the interviews.

I must also thank the Center for the Study of Public Scholarship and the Rockefeller Foundation for allowing me the time and the opportunity to write up the interviews and to bring the book up to the "completed first draft" phase.

In addition, I would like to thank a whole range of people who supported me in one way or another. Foremost among these is Robyn Kleinschmidt, who showed a maturity way beyond her years in managing my affairs for so many years. I also have to thank Yazeed Kamaldien, then a freelance South African journalist, and Elizabeth Langton, an American student intern, who assisted me with much of the research and initial legwork.

I must thank the Reverend Kent "Buck" Bellmore, for being a friend and a family member for me in Atlanta, for reading the first drafts and giving me comments; and AJ Cilliers, who assisted with proofreading.

I would also like to thank George Hallett, one of South Africa's foremost photographers, for undertaking this labour of love with me. Both of us learnt a lot about identity and racial issues in the process of doing the interviews. George has managed to capture the essential elements of a range of different personalities in his intriguing photographs.

I want to thank Archbishop Emeritus Desmond Tutu for agreeing to write the foreword to this book and also for his support throughout the years.

I want to thank the publishers for believing in me and this book and I also want to thank my editor, Bronwyn McLennan, for working against almost impossible deadlines.

I also need to thank all the people who agreed to be interviewed. I know that all of them, like me, are grappling to find answers to the issues of race and racism, and the interviews could not have been easy for any of them.

Finally, but definitely not the least important, I want to thank my wife, Ibtisaan, and my daughters, Nadia, Raisa and Larah, for being the best family in the world. They have stood by me through good and bad and I love all of them very, very much. I would not be able to do anything without the knowledge that I have their love and support.

FOREWORD

When Ryland Fisher approached me a few years ago and told me that he was writing this book, I thought he was a little bit crazy. This was not a job to be approached lightly and, irrespective of how you approached it, it was bound to upset some people.

The issue of race and racism in post-apartheid South Africa is not one on which there is unanimity. Depending on who you speak to, everything is either hunky-dory in South Africa or things are heading for a calamity.

There are certain things in Fisher's book with which I do not agree, but I am aware that his intention was not to have everyone agree with everything he wrote. I believe his intention was to stimulate discussion and debate, and I think the book succeeds in doing just that.

The fact that it is a journalistic book and not an academic one is also important. Too often debates on issues such as race and racism are restricted to lofty academic halls and do not reach the masses of people who are affected. One would hope that this book will reach a few more people besides academics.

If there is one area where I could fault this book, it is that there could possibly have been a bit more diversity in the interview subjects, but then again it is not always possible to please everyone, and it would be difficult to ensure that everyone in South Africa felt represented in this book.

Ultimately, this book is but a starting point for a much-needed discussion on race. Read it, and let's start talking.

Desmond Tutu
Archbishop Emeritus

INTRODUCTION
I AM NOT A RACIST, BUT ...

In South Africa the term "racist" conjures up a certain image: that of a white man with a thick beard and a weathered face dressed in a khaki uniform and perhaps even sporting a comb in his sock.

Most South Africans used to believe that black people were not capable of being racist, because this implied a sense of power and the ability to act on one's beliefs. This was the case for many years in South Africa, while a white minority used its economic and political power to oppress the majority. It is possible that this situation has changed now that black people have political power. However, economic power is still held largely by white people, while most black people remain poor.

I want to challenge the assumption of the typical racist, because I believe that I am a racist. I say this even though I do not fit the typical stereotype of a South African racist. Moreover, I believe that most people in South Africa are racists.

I mention this reluctantly and not at all lightly. I mention this not to shock, but because it is a fact. I believe that I am a racist because my entire life I have been groomed to become one:

• I was born in the non-white section of a maternity hospital in Cape Town, South Africa.

• I grew up in the coloureds-only townships of the Cape Flats in the 1960s and 1970s.

1

- I attended coloureds-only schools.

- For most of my young life, I socialised only with coloured people. The first time I interacted with white people was when I went to a white university, which people like me could attend only if we had special government permission. My interaction with African people was equally minimal until, as a teenager, I became interested in politics. I then went into an African township for the first time in my life.

- I could only go to non-white beaches, which were normally the worst beaches because most of the best beaches in South Africa were reserved for whites.

- I had to enter shops through the back door or through a special entrance reserved for non-whites.

- I could only swim in municipal swimming pools reserved for non-white people.

- I could not go to the theatre, because the theatre was for white people only.

- The term "reserved for whites" became a part of our everyday vocabulary.

- I could not become a pilot, which was my ambition in life, because only white people could become pilots. People like me could become preachers or teachers, or maybe accountants.

- I voted for the first time, for a democratic government, when I was 34 years old. Before that, I was not allowed to vote because only white people were allowed to vote.

- I grew up in South Africa, where race and racism has dominated our society for much of the last century and continues to dominate our society today.

For almost 50 years, from 1948 until 1994, the official government policy of our country was based on race, racism and racial separation. We had a host of laws regulating our lives, such as the Population Registration Act (which defined people according to race groups), the Group Areas Act (which determined where we could live), the Immorality Act (which

2

prevented love and sex across the colour line) and the Mixed Marriages Act (which prevented marriages across the colour line).

I grew up in the era of apartheid and the stigma of that era will probably stay with me forever. To this day, I still find myself having preconceived notions of Africans, whites, Indians or coloured people, who form the major race groups in South Africa. It is because of this that I say that I am a racist.

But if I am a racist, I am not a passive acceptor of my racism. I am prepared to own up to my racism and I am doing my best to fight against it. Like the people in Alcoholics Anonymous, I believe that one must admit to one's faults before one can start to deal with them. Failure to admit to one's faults will mean that one will probably die with those faults. The difference between me and the people who are not prepared to admit to their racism is that I will probably overcome my racism at some point in my life.

In South Africa today it is difficult to find people, especially in the white community, who will admit to being racist now or in the past. And despite the fact that the National Party remained in power, by overwhelming majorities in all the all-white elections between 1948 and 1994, it is difficult to find anyone who will admit to having voted for them.

Similarly, one often hears people saying, "I am not a racist, but ..." and then proceeding to make racist comments. To those people I always say: "I am a racist, but ..." and then I explain why I say that I am a racist.

In his autobiography, *Makes Me Wanna Holler (A Young Black Man in America)*, Nathan McCall writes about a conversation he had with a white friend who asked him why he thought about race all the time.

I told Danny I did not have a choice in the matter. "You can sit around and intellectualize about race when you want to, and when you get tired of it you can set it aside and go surfing or hang-gliding and forget about it. But I can't. Race affects every facet of my life, man. I can't get past race because white folks won't let me get past it. They remind me of it everywhere I go. Every time I step into an elevator and a white woman bunches up in the corner like she thinks I wanna rape her, I'm forced to think about it. Every time I walk into the stores, the suspicious looks in white shopkeepers' eyes make me think about it. Every time I walk past whites sitting in their cars, I hear the door locks clicking and I think about it. I can't get away from it, man. I stay so mad all the time because I am forced to spend so much time and energy reacting to race. I hate it. It wearies me. But there is no escape, man. No escape."

In many ways, McCall's experience mirrors my own. I too am obsessed with race, but only because race has always been obsessed with me.

Steve Biko and beyond

Over the years, I have dealt with my own racism in different ways. When I was introduced to the thoughts and writings of Stephen Bantu Biko in the 1970s, I embraced them immediately.

Biko's writings told me that I was no longer coloured or non-white, but black. His writing told me that black was something beautiful, something to be proud of. Biko argued that white should not necessarily always be the standard against which everything else gets judged. He believed that we should no longer accept the term "non-white". Why, Biko asked, could whites not be called "non-blacks"?

I identified with this thinking and I began to actively pursue news about the African community in South Africa. I wanted to find out what it was like to be black, not only in name, but also in deed.

I sympathised with the people in Soweto, and in the 1980s, I began to read papers such as *City Press* and the *Sowetan* (newspapers aimed at the African community) to learn what was happening in Soweto and to begin to understand the pulse of our nation. For the first time in my life, I felt part of the black majority and no longer part of an unidentifiable group of people called "coloured".

Later on I was introduced to non-racialism, a term which accepted the distinction between blacks and whites, but did not emphasise them in the way that Biko had. This term, I think, was introduced to accommodate whites who were sympathetic to our cause. This was also one of the great distinctions between the Black Consciousness Movement, as espoused by people such as Biko, and the policies of the African National Congress.

Recently, however, I have noticed that people who used to accept me as black now refer to me as coloured and, by that action, exclude me and others who may or may not look like me from the majority of South Africans once again.

No easy answers

The aim of this book is not to provide answers, but to present some interesting questions that can contribute to the debate around race and racism in South Africa.

It is important to start this debate. Since the release from prison of Nelson Mandela and since South Africa became a democracy, there are many people in our country who believe that, because apartheid is a thing of the past, racism too is a thing of the past.

Yet racism remains a minefield in our society, and if it is not dealt with properly, it has the potential to become explosive.

Most white people in South Africa feel uncomfortable when one raises the topic of racism. Maybe it has to do with guilt over what happened under apartheid, or perhaps it is a genuine attempt at forgetting the past.

Yet it is difficult to forget the past when its legacies still loom very large in our society. Every now and again, something happens that reminds us that racism is still with us. A hotel refuses to accept black clients, a hairdresser refuses to employ a black person because most of its clientele is white, a white Springbok rugby player refuses to share a room with a black player, a white barber refuses to cut the hair of the black chairperson of South Africa's Human Rights Commission, and a black schoolgirl gets violently assaulted by a fellow white schoolgirl assisted by her mother and boyfriend.

But the greater effects of our racist past can been seen every day in the many townships where black people continue to live the same miserable lives they lived under apartheid and where our democratic government is building worse houses for poor people than those built by the apartheid government.

The effects can be seen in the large numbers of unemployed people who walk the streets of our cities, knowing that they will never find work, because nobody is taking the responsibility to create jobs.

They can be seen in the fact that the number of black-owned and controlled companies on the Johannesburg Securities Exchange has actually dwindled over the past few years.

They can be seen in the fact that the government has had to intervene to legislate on employment equity and black economic empowerment because most white companies would not change and open up to blacks unless they were forced to do so.

When one looks at the youth, however, there is some hope. My daughters have been going to what we call "former Model C schools" for many years now, and they have friends who come from all racial backgrounds. A while ago, one of my daughters had three of her best friends sleep over at our house. As they played together, the racist in me suddenly realised that they represented the "Rainbow Nation", as Archbishop Emeritus Desmond Tutu coined South African society. They were white, African, coloured and Indian. And they were not even aware of it. That is what I call progress and that is what gives me hope for the future of South Africa.

CHAPTER 1
RACE IN THE NOT-SO-NEW SOUTH AFRICA

What this book tries to do

In compiling the research for this book, and while conducting the interviews, I discovered that the issues around race and racism in South Africa are not clear-cut; in fact, they are extremely complex. Rather than reaching any neat conclusions, I left each of the interviews feeling more confused than ever. The objective of this book is to share some of this confusion with readers, and, with the help of the people I interviewed, to serve as a catalyst for many more discussions around the issues of race and racism.

The book is written from the perspective of someone who has always been committed to the struggle for liberation in South Africa, someone who still believes in the words of the Freedom Charter, a document adopted in 1955, which said that "South Africa shall belong to all who live in it, black and white". I believe that I am still true to those ideals of non-racialism. However, I feel there are many people in our society who have forgotten those words, and that this is contributing to the racism we are experiencing in South Africa today.

This book comes at an important time in our country's history. Just over ten years since our first democratic elections, we are now at a point where the initial euphoria has died down and the government has to start delivering. Yet how much can the government deliver and how much can it continue to blame apartheid for today's problems?

Several other issues are covered in this book, but it tries to end on a hopeful note, where it looks at how we should explain apartheid to our youth and whether we can instil anti-racist values in them.

Introducing the interviewees

The various chapters in the book are based on a series of interviews I did over the past few years with prominent and not-so-prominent South Africans. The interviewees are not a representative sample of the South African population and this book is by no means a scientific study of race and racism in South Africa. Overall, however, I believe that the group I interviewed represent an interesting mix of people with pertinent views about a crucial debate in our society.

In keeping with the non-academic nature of this book, all interviewees are referred to by their first names rather than their surnames. I have not included excerpts from each person in every chapter, and have not asked every interviewee the same questions. The interviews are not represented in any particular order, so as to avoid giving the impression that any one person is more important than the other. It should also be noted that most of these interviews were conducted in 2002; therefore, some of the people may have slightly or radically altered their views since then. As far as possible, I have tried to let the people I interviewed speak without any interference from me, and to represent the interviews in their own words.

This chapter introduces the people I interviewed and some of their views on issues that are important to them. They also relate some of their personal experiences of racism. In this chapter I have presented their responses in alphabetical order.

Vincent Barnes
Vincent Barnes is the assistant coach of the South African national cricket team. At the time of the interview, he was joint coach of the Western Province cricket team.

Vincent attended Livingstone High School in Claremont, Cape Town, after which he did his apprenticeship as a fitter and turner at the naval dockyard in Simonstown. "It was very traumatic for me as an anti-apartheid sportsman in those years to work at the dockyard [South Africa's navy at the time was all-white]. I eventually left because I could not stand it. I got involved in sport and sales. I first worked for a sporting company and then went to work for Old Mutual [one of South Africa's biggest financial services companies]."

In the apartheid days, there was a prominent non-racial sports administrator called Hassan Howa, who used to say that there could be no normal sport in an abnormal society. I asked Vincent whether he believed that our society had reached the point where it could be called a normal society.

"In certain areas, it has reached that point. I don't think cricket is far from it. We had a period where unity was more about being allowed to play international cricket and everybody was happy. But I think we have paid the price for that, for not transforming the sport fast enough. For instance, those of us who played on the non-racial side struggled for a long time to get our statistics recognised and they only recently agreed to recognise them.

"The white guys used to talk about playing so many tests, yet we were never allowed to play test cricket. I did not think that the so-called international cricket that white South Africans played in the 1970s and 1980s should have been recognised as test cricket. When we had unity, everyone should have started with zero. What happens in the future is going to be important. There is still a mainly white norm in cricket, but that is changing slowly. Slowly it is becoming fifty-fifty.

"With me being coach, I know it has an effect on making black players feel a lot more comfortable. I understand how difficult it is for black players to perform in these teams. There was a case a few years ago when one of the black players went home after the day's play and witnessed his cousin murder one of his friends. The next day he just came back to play and was expected to perform at the same level as the day before.

"White people actually don't understand that there is no support structure for these players in the townships. For instance, when black players come to practice, you have to accept that they cannot bring their kit with them from the township, so they leave their kit at the office here. They cannot travel with their kit in a minibus taxi. There is always a chance that they could be robbed.

"We need to involve more black people in the upper structures of cricket to make sure that we have more people who understand. When you have somebody who understands at the top, you find that the players are much more comfortable."

Vincent related some of his experiences of racism in the sports arena. "Last year we played against Northerns and in the match prior to ours, they played a [white] youngster who got the man of the match award. He got left out of the match against us and they lost badly against us. The reports in the newspapers the next day said that this youngster was left out because of the quota system.

"I phoned the reporter who wrote this and said I was not going to accept that they were trying to put a damper on our victory, by claiming that we won because of the quota system. I said that they had played another white player who was actually useless and they could have played the youngster in his place. Instead they told everybody that they were playing a player of colour ahead of this player and that is why they lost against Western Province.

"If these kinds of things happen, if they rear their head, I tackle them right away. I always seem to be the one dealing with any sensitive issue where a person of colour has a problem."

Carel Boshoff

Carel Boshoff IV is a descendant of a leading Afrikaner family. He runs Orania, an Afrikaner homeland that was established in 1991 in the Northern Cape Province, shortly before South Africa became a democracy. He is a member of the Northern Cape legislature on behalf of the right-wing Freedom Front political party.

Carel grew up in a traditional Afrikaner home in Pretoria. His father was a missionary and a professor. Carel studied philosophy at the University of Pretoria. "I wanted to find the relationship between the theory and the practice of philosophy," he explained. "From a young age, because of the context of my family and environment, I developed a certain consciousness of Afrikaner thought and the identity that was linked to it. As a young student, I became involved in attempts to creatively review this identity. My experience has been that some things are pre-destined with regards to your personal and group identity, but this notion raises a whole lot of issues. I was involved in a group of students who tried to take this concept of self-destiny further, while not agreeing with the regime of P. W. Botha, but also not being associated with the struggle. We were looking at a sort of reconfirmation of the Afrikaner idea within a morally more justifiable set-up."

I remarked that there were people who would accuse him of being racist for wanting to live in a separate area such as Orania, which is effectively a white homeland.

"We probably have to understand where that criticism comes from, but I don't believe people are aware of or understand my thinking, so they don't know quite how to respond to me. There are many towns and settlements in South Africa that are mono-cultural and that consist only of a single race, language or cultural group, and no fingers are pointed at those communities. I think one of the reasons people tend to be critical of a community such as Orania is because it also has social and economic benefits that allow such a group to retain its economic privileges, and it encourages the protection of those privileges.

"My view of these things is slightly different. My image and experience of Orania is that we are dealing with a community that is finding itself in the middle of a changing relationship with the whole. The key word here is probably marginalisation.

"This community used to find itself in the centre of state administration and decision making and, as such, used to present itself over the whole of South Africa as an administration class or a ruling class. It used to have a presence in every little town and now this community is finding that even in those places, it has become a minority that no longer stands in the centre. At the same time, it does not have anywhere near as high a concentration of people as other population or language groups.

"Now there are different strategies for Afrikaners. The one is to simply, on an individual level, try to see to oneself. This is manifested in the emigration to foreign countries of those who can afford to do so. But there is also that immigration internally to a world of closed walls – the security villages that the middle class have now created for themselves.

"For me, Orania is an attempt to establish a local community and I am very honest about this. I would love to see more of these communities established in South Africa – local communities with a certain cultural expression and the institutional framework necessary to protect them. I hope that the practice of these communities will prove not to be racist and that the representatives of this kind of thinking will present themselves to the open forums that South Africa offers and be understood and accepted not to be racist. People must begin to see that all we are trying to do is to provide people with a safe place to stay. We want to provide Afrikaners with a place to live among their own people, but we need to destroy the myth that translates their actions with racism."

I commented that it was very difficult not to see Orania in racist terms. I asked Carel, for instance, whether they would open Orania to so-called brown Afrikaners. "The answer is not 'no'," he responded, "The answer is that we are placing this whole undertaking within the framework of the Constitution and we are motivating that this includes the right of people to move within South Africa and to live where they want to."

I asked him whether there were any English-speaking people in Orania. He replied "yes" and I asked him how he reconciled this with being an Afrikaner. "The community functions on the basis of a central agreement. For instance, Afrikaans is the language we use in Orania, whether you go to the shop or to school; wherever you go. An English-speaking person who comes to Orania and wants to speak English and also wants his education in English will not be received very sympathetically. In other words, it is about fitting in to the community."

I said that it appeared to me that it was easier for the people of Orania to accept English-speaking whites than it was to accept Afrikaans-speaking coloureds.

"It is an historic thing that goes back to the politics of the twentieth century. The Union of South Africa that was brought into being with violence consisted of white politics to the exclusion of the non-white sectors. It is easy to look back and to say that Afrikaners formed a majority within the white community of South Africa. That is why it was logical that if Afrikaners could mobilise their interests properly, then they could also control the state institutions. If they did that, then they could sort out their problems, including the poor white question. In this process they had to find a way of cooperating with the English-speaking white community who represented the rest of the voters. It was necessary and in their favour to involve English-speaking whites who were interested in their political projects.

"This becomes very clear, especially around the formation of the Republic in 1961. When the question of whether South Africa should stay within the Commonwealth came up, there was a definite attempt to reconcile the differences between Afrikaners and English-speaking whites. This was necessary to achieve success in the referendum over whether South Africa should become a republic or not. People got assurances with relation to the Commonwealth, and in relation to their own existence. This led to a concept that became understandable and not uncommon: the concept of a kind of white nation."

I asked him what would happen if the social experiment in Orania did not work. "If Orania does not work in the way that it should work, then we will do something else. But at least we are coming up with a creative response to our situation. And we will remain busy; we will remain busy trying to find answers to our situation."

Asked whether he had any personal experiences of racism to relate, Carel could not think of any "spectacular examples".

"Nobody has ever beaten me up because I am white. However, I do experience subtle references all the time, when people hint about things on a racist level.

"I don't reduce everything to racism, however, so I don't always accept these references as racism. If someone thinks I am an arsehole, then it is normally because I am different to him, and so this is not necessarily racism. I have had experiences where people have rejected me for being too intellectual, for instance. The point is that I experience these negative comments as often among white people as I do among black people, so I have never linked them to racism.

Phatekile Holomisa

Nkosi Sango Phatekile Holomisa is the president of the Congress of Traditional Leaders of South Africa (Contralesa), which is the major organisation representing South Africa's traditional leaders. He is also an advocate of the High Court, a Member of Parliament for the ruling party, and chairperson of the Steering Committee of the SADC Council of Traditional Leaders.

Phatekile was born in Mqanduli in the Eastern Cape in August 1959. His parents, Chief Mathatisa Moses Holomisa and Nkosikazi Nokupila Phyllis Holomisa, were both royalty. "My father and his father were Thembu chiefs and my mother's father was also a chief of the Thembu tribe," said Phatekile. "I am the leader of the AmaHegebe [Thembu tribe] because I am the leader of the ruling clan of the tribe. For this reason, I am also the cultural and religious leader of the AmaHegebe.

"I was about two years old when I was taken away to a place called Idutywa in the Transkei, to the home of my mother's aunt, but she died when I was about five years old. That is where I grew up and where I lived until I completed my LLB.

"At university I was involved in student political activities such as the Azanian Students Organisation [Azaso] and the Black Students Society [BSS], of which I was the deputy president. The BSS was the SRC [Student Representative Council] equivalent for black students at the time. I was also active in UDF [United Democratic Front] activities, so I knew what was happening.

"In 1984, when I realised that I was about to complete my studies, I wanted to know what advice the ANC would give me regarding my position as a traditional leader. My father was a traditional leader and he died when my grandfather was still alive in 1972.

"I had to make sure that I did not misuse the money for my studies, because when I was at university, my fees were paid for by my tribe.

In a way, I was educated by them. They said that because I was a bachelor at the time, I could not take up the position. However, being married was not strictly required by my custom at the time; it was an act of subterfuge by my uncle who did not want to vacate the position.

"I did not mind because it allowed me time to establish myself as a legal practitioner. I was still serving my articles at the time and it was decided that I should come to Umtata to set up a practice as an advocate. This would help to facilitate my activities with the ANC."

Phatekile opened his practice in 1989 and became involved in Contralesa shortly thereafter. He practised until 1994 when he went to Parliament.

I asked him how Parliament had changed since the 1994 elections and what major problems were involved in this transformation. "We came to a Parliament that had its own rules and regulations, and we were informed by the culture that we found here. We had to use those rules and regulations. We are gradually changing them, but it is taking a long time.

"I don't think there is enough boldness on the part of those who should be driving the process of transforming this institution. We are still basically a white European institution, besides the fact that the Africans are in the majority now. Maybe it has to do with the gripe that I have with government for failing to allow traditional leaders to be part of this institution.

"Even though we have a House of Traditional Leaders nationally and provincially, their views are not taken seriously. There is no serious mechanism aimed at channelling their views into what is happening here in Parliament. It is still being done haphazardly and gradually.

"Beyond that, the Africans are in the majority in Parliament and now and again we speak our language when we address Parliament. However, in the main it is Eurocentric. We speak English, and there is not even translation into Xhosa. There are standing translations into English and Afrikaans, but there is no standing translation into Xhosa, Venda, Zulu, Shangaan or the other languages, and there is no excuse for that. We should be able to speak our languages and have a translation service so that we can listen to any speech in our own language.

"Even on the day that there was a debate around the use of language, there was no translation into all the languages. Most of the people, even while espousing the use of other languages, were speaking English. Also, when you are speaking your language, some of the other racial groups think what you are saying is not important. They argue that if it was important you would have wanted them to hear it directly from yourself and not through translations. They don't listen to you unless you speak English."

Khusta and Karen Jack

Mkhuseli "Khusta" was a key leader of the anti-apartheid movement in the 1980s. He is now a prominent Eastern Cape businessman.

Khusta was born in Humansdorp in the Eastern Cape, the second last of eight children. His family was evicted from a farm on the Gamtoos River when he was about four years old. Khusta told me about how he was kicked out of high school in Port Elizabeth: "I had to go to Port Elizabeth to do Standard Seven [Grade Nine], and ended up with a problem. I did not have what they used to call a family card. The Bantu Administration Board regulated the stay of some people in the township through a system called the family card. When you went to school, you had to produce a family card. If you did not have it, you would be kicked out. I got kicked out with a lot of other people. From that point onwards, I became involved in politics. Before that I did not know what politics meant. That was in 1975."

In 1979, Khusta became a founder member of the Congress of South African Students (Cosas) and in 1982 he founded and was made the first president of the Port Elizabeth Youth Congress. He also became deeply involved in the emerging civic organisations and later the UDF, which he served as publicity secretary from 1990. He was elected chairman of the Port Elizabeth Consumer Boycott Committee in 1985. In the early 1990s, he earned an honour's degree in Economics and Development Studies at Sussex University in Britain.

I asked Khusta whether he'd experienced much racism in his life and, if so, how he had dealt with it. He said that in his businesses, he employed people who came from different political and even military backgrounds. "I employ hard guys. Some were in Koevoet [an apartheid-supporting anti-terrorism army unit], some were in MK [the military wing of the ANC], and some were in APLA [the military wing of the Pan Africanist Congress]. I talk to all of them. The black guys would sometimes come to me to complain about some of the white guys and they would bring up the fact that they were in Koevoet. I would tell them this did not matter to me. If you have a job to do, and you stick to the specifications, then I don't care whether you have a Koevoet background or whether you have an AWB [Afrikanerweerstandsbeweging] background.

"All the people who work for me really enjoy working for me, because when somebody comes to complain over racial issues, I can handle it. I can solve those kinds of problems because of my political skills and understanding of what racism is and how to deal with it. I explain to people why I need to have white people, coloured people and Indian people in my business. I want to reflect South Africa. What threatens many people is when you do not explain to them what you want to achieve. You have to explain things such as black economic empowerment. You have to give people your reasons for doing things."

Karen Jack was born in Cape Town. Her father was an Anglican minister. "When I was about ten, my father was elected Bishop of Port Elizabeth, so we moved to Port Elizabeth. I completed my schooling at a girls-only religious school. My family was always considered sort of liberal. Both my brothers were in the ANC underground, and my father always used to be outspoken about the security police. We used to get hammers and sickles painted on our walls. Coming from that kind of background helped me later in my relationship with Khusta.

"After school I went overseas for a year and then to Rhodes University. I did not finish there, because I went to work as a journalist. I met Khusta on the day he got out of detention in 1989. I was reporting on the release of the detainees for the East Cape News Agency."

I asked Karen about her personal experiences of racism. "At our children's school, we push for more blacks to be on the governing board, or we complain about our local press which has got a lot of racist articles in it," she said. "We will voice opinions like that, but to us, personally, we don't get to deal with a lot of racism."

Wilmot James

Doctor Wilmot James is the executive director of the African Genome Education Institute and Honorary Professor in the Division of Genetics, Faculty of Health Sciences at the University of Cape Town. He is chairman of the Immigration Advisory Board of South Africa, and a trustee of the Ford Foundation of New York, the Impumelelo Innovations Awards Programme, the US-SA Centre for Leadership and Public Values and the Cape Philharmonic Orchestra. He is a non-executive director of Sanlam Limited, Sanlam Life and Media24. Dr James was formerly an executive director of the Human Sciences Research Council, a dean of humanities at the University of Cape Town, executive director of the Institute for Democracy of South Africa (Idasa) and a professor of sociology at the University of Cape Town. He has written extensively on issues related to race and racism in South Africa and abroad.

Wilmot was born in Paarl, a rural town in the Western Cape, in July 1953. "I spent almost ten years in Paarl, living opposite a farm, before my parents moved to Cape Town in 1961," he said. "I spent my teenage years in Athlone living at Hewat Training College because my parents were the house parents at the student hostel. I really grew up in the Athlone area, living between Belgravia and Thornton Road. I went to Athlone High School. My parents were teachers and they were part of the Paarl Unity Movement network. [The Unity Movement was a political organisation that believed in non-collaboration with the apartheid government.]

"After high school, I worked at a warehouse as a casual book packer for a year and then I went to the University of the Western Cape [UWC] in 1971. I left UWC in 1976 with an honour's degree in Sociology."

I asked him how he was able to make a difference to society in his role as an executive director of the HSRC, the position he held at the time of the interview. "I don't see enough support, celebration and appreciation of the people who excel, and particularly black people who excel. The project that I am responsible for is partly doing biographical research on people who excel in terms of leadership in the arts and sports.

"Also, as a country and as a continent, I don't believe that we are in touch in the way we should be with major developments in science. The most important development over the last few years has been the human genome project, which is an effort to investigate our genetic material. We will have a detailed understanding and a map of our genetics and our chemical infrastructure. It is important for us to engage with this in terms of legal aspects regarding intellectual property rights and who owns that information. There are also major ethical questions around equity and access to that information. The short answer is that there are a whole lot of broad demands and challenges out there that I could research at the Human Science Research Council in an attempt to provide answers to all these questions."

I asked him what could be done to get more black people interested in mathematics and science. "There is a general problem that science is very badly taught at school. Science is immensely exciting, but at school it is taught in a very dull way. And the teaching of mathematics has always been, in my own experience, a very daunting thing. *Ons was bang vir wiskunde* [We were scared of mathematics]. Most people thought that maths was difficult to learn.

"Black children have a long history of not being taught maths and science at all. We now have 120 pilot schools for maths and science and it is expanding more and more. That is why we need more teachers trained to teach maths and science. It has to become a solid part of the curriculum at schools. I think the Department of Education is trying to do something about this.

"The teacher training has to focus on the ethos of making science and mathematics exciting, up to date and vibrant. We also need to attract more black teachers."

Wilmot said he'd had many personal experiences of racism over the years. As an example, he related the following incident.

"I was about 16 years old and my older brother was driving

my father's car. A white guy bashed into our car while my brother was dropping off my girlfriend at about 2 a.m. The white guy was completely in the wrong and when we went to court, he pleaded guilty. However, his whole defence was about us being coloured and therefore drunk. He was convicted and the magistrate said he had never met two more honest boys than us."

Wilmot said that if he had a personal problem with racism, he would speak out about it. "But one always worries that you are overreacting or have a chip on your shoulder. You should have a balanced response to life. People might not intend to be racist, and yet you perceive it that way. I am also really open to talking to people, no matter how racist they might or might not be."

Rhoda Kadalie

Rhoda Kadalie, the granddaughter of a prominent ANC-aligned unionist of the 1950s, is a human rights activist who has been particularly critical of South Africa's ruling party. She is currently the executive director of Impumelelo Innovations and Awards Trust, which aims to reward innovative government and civil society initiatives that improve social delivery in the eradication of poverty. She is also a former member of South Africa's Human Rights Commission.

Rhoda grew up in District Six. "I am the daughter of very mixed parentage. My father was a priest in District Six, working among the gangsters in the community. He was the son of a Malawian, Clements Kadalie [founder of the Industrial and Commercial Workers Union (ICU)]. Clements came to South Africa and married a Malay descendant, my grandmother. My mother's mother was a rural coloured woman from Bredasdorp and her father was a white railway worker. I married a German man at the age of 28, and I have a daughter who is also mixed in many ways. In terms of race, I am a thoroughbred mongrel, which I find an asset in the political landscape of South Africa.

Rhoda spoke about how her family was forcibly removed from Mowbray when it was declared a white area. "I went to five different schools because of the Group Areas Act. After we were evicted from Mowbray I went to Sidney Street Primary in Woodstock. At first they wouldn't let me in because I was not white enough. All the coloured kids that went there were very white. But my parents made a case for my academic credentials and I got in purely on my results.

"After matric I applied to study physiotherapy at UCT, but at the time there was a requirement to submit a full-length photograph of yourself in a bathing costume. I refused to do that and, under protest, went to UWC, which in retrospect I don't regret, because I think my political formation was achieved there. I did a four-year degree in Library Science. I then majored in English and Anthropology, and continued my post-graduate studies in Anthropology at UWC and UCT. I then went to Holland to do a master's in Development Studies."

I asked her if she ever discovered the reason behind UCT's request for applicants to submit photos of themselves in bathing costumes. "I think it was semi-racist at the time. They said they had to see how fit and proper you were to do physiotherapy. I wrote about this in a newspaper article, and Helen Zille, who was then public affairs director at UCT, disputed it and said that I was misrepresenting UCT. She went to investigate and had to apologise because it was indeed so. UCT was very embarrassed about it. I had a hunch at the time that it was a way to shift the wheat from the chaff. It could have had racial implications."

Asked why she had left the Human Rights Commission, she replied, "I left the HRC very reluctantly, because it was a job made in heaven for me. It was a job I went into with trepidation and I was amazed that I mastered it. I left because of the racial politics. Also, it was a place where affirmative action went wrong. Black people were appointed to key positions and they were not able to do the job. Because these people were not able to do the job, they appointed even more people.

"We became a bloated structure purely on the basis of non-delivery and incompetence. When people like me and the other commissioners who were not black would question these appointments, we would be blamed as racist. It is an organisation that has absorbed a lot of taxpayers' money. The reason I left was because the taxpayer was not getting value for money. We were all riding the gravy train with enormous salaries and perks, but with very little filtered back to the community."

I asked her to relate some personal experiences of racism.

"I experienced racism in public life like everybody else, such as not being able to use separate amenities. I was thrown off Muizenberg Beach once. I couldn't swim because I had smashed my toe and I was waiting for my husband. The white cops sent the black cop to tell me to move and I said I wouldn't move. I asked the black cop why he was on the beach as a black cop and he got all exasperated. I then said, 'In any case, I can't leave because my husband is over there.' So they told me to wait for my husband. When he came, they saw that he was white, and they didn't know what to do.

"I can regale you with a hundred and one stories. You go into shops and immediately the antennae of the security are alerted and they watch you. You get that all the time. I go into a fancy shop in Dean Street in Newlands [an affluent suburb in Cape Town], and the shop assistants won't even look up. A white woman will come in and they will immediately ask to help her. The assumption is you cannot afford to shop there. I have to deal with this kind of racism all the time."

Kenny and Sielie Nolan
Kenny and Sielie Nolan live in Manenberg, one of the poorest neighbourhoods on the Cape Flats. There are huge murals on the walls of their block of flats, depicting American rap musicians Tupac Shakur and Snoop Doggy Dog. One of the Western Cape's most notorious gangs, the Hard Livings Kids, used to have their headquarters across the road.

Kenny Nolan was born in Vasco in Cape Town. His family later moved to Kensington where he grew up and attended school until Standard Four [Grade Six], when he left to help his father earn money for their household. Kenny was 49 when I interviewed him in early 2002. He was not working at the time, having lost his job a few years before. Manenberg has a high unemployment rate, which is typical of many of the townships on the Cape Flats. "I have a little stall where we sell stuff to the local people, and sometimes I work at the school, but most of the time I do not have work," Kenny explained.

Gwendolene "Sielie" Nolan was born in Kewtown on the Cape Flats. She attended school at Modderdam High School in Bonteheuwel until Standard Six (Grade Eight). She was 46 at the time of the interview. "I was 14 when I had to go and work in a leather factory. I worked there for 25 years until the factory closed down and I was retrenched. I sat at home for three years, but for the last three years I have been doing a bit of domestic work three days a week."

I asked the Nolans whether they had been affected by the Group Areas Act. "No," answered Kenny. "We lived for a while with my family in the docks cottages near the city centre. My uncle and aunt lived there because they worked on the railways. Everything was plentiful at the time. We had no problem with food or money, but now things are very different."

I asked them how the previous government had succeeded in dividing people. Kenny responded, "I don't know how they did it, but I remember that when we were children the black people lived with us in one area. That was before places like Langa were built. This was in Kensington in the 1950s. We all lived together, blacks and coloureds. Then they opened Langa and they removed all the black people from Kensington. So then black people had their own areas, such as Langa and Nyanga. There were also coloured people who were forcibly removed from areas such as Constantia."

I asked them what language people spoke in the days when Africans and coloureds were living together in the same areas. "We spoke a mix of Afrikaans, English and Xhosa. Everything was mixed together," said Kenny. Sielie said she was trying to learn Xhosa: "When I travel in the taxi, I learn that one says 'enkosi' for 'thank you', and if you should not get change, you say 'ayiko ichange'. For children, they say 'abantwana'. The way I see black people is that they are very friendly. They like to talk. They don't need to know each other to strike up a conversation. It is not the same with coloured people. And if you can reply to them in their own language, they are very impressed. Sometimes on the taxi I say I want to get off at the *abantwana* crossing and then the lady next to me will say '*abantwana*' and everyone laughs in appreciation.

"One needs to learn to know them to understand them. I think if we got rid of apartheid and racism, South Africa would be a much better place. If we really became a rainbow nation, things would be a lot easier for all of us."

Kenny said coloureds were more divided than Africans. "Coloureds divide themselves into Muslims and Christians, people with straight hair and people with curly hair. You don't find these divisions among black people."

I asked them whether the apartheid government used language to divide people. "The government used their brains and did their homework," said Sielie, "They built Langa and Nyanga on one side of the railway line. You have blacks on the one side of the railway line and coloureds on the other side. If you look at the way people lived in District Six, things were very different. Yes, there were gangsters there too, but at least people did not live on top of each other. Now we have forty-eight families in a block of flats without even space for the children to play. We have just been dumped here." There are twelve people living in the Nolans' two-bedroom apartment.

Asked if they could remember any particular instances of racism under apartheid, Sielie said: "I remember how we had to sit upstairs in the bus while the white people sat at the bottom. I also remember running to the third class or the non-white first class coaches on the train. Sometimes we would miss the train because we could only reach the white first-class coach and we were not allowed on. Even at the unemployment office, the whites would stand in one queue while the coloureds and Africans would stand in another queue."

"Of course," said Kenny, "we were also not allowed to go to white beaches. We were stopped many times from going onto white beaches."

Asked how he dealt with people who made racist comments towards him, Kenny said: "I normally just tell them, 'It's fine. I am a Hotnot and I am proud to be a Hotnot.'"

Sielie made an example of how hair texture featured in racist and derogatory comments among coloured people. "Some of our neighbours are Muslim and the others are Christian. One neighbour said to his wife, 'You see, those people are Christians, but they have better hair than the Muslims.'

"Hair texture is very important in the coloured community. And Muslims are supposed to have better hair than Christians. If you have a child with blonde hair, like my granddaughter, then people will start talking and saying that it is the child of a white man. Maybe it is the boss's child. This is the way people talk here. But we can't be held accountable for the things our forefathers did."

Trevor Oosterwyk

Trevor Oosterwyk was a journalist at the *Cape Argus* at the time of the interview. He is a former UDF and ANC activist and a former historian at the University of the Western Cape. He was the ANC's election coordinator in Mitchells Plain in 1994, after which he started a cultural movement called the December 1st Movement, which aimed to mobilise coloured people on behalf of the ANC. He now works for Statistics SA in Pretoria.

"I was born in March 1958 in Bridgetown, the second of nine children," said Trevor. "My parents got a house from the [Cape Town City] Council in Bonteheuwel when the area was built in 1960. I lived there from the time I was about two years old until September 1979, when we moved to Mitchells Plain.

"My life was pretty much an ordinary working-class life. We were poor. More often than not we did not know where the next meal was coming from. We could never buy fancy clothes; we could never buy school shoes. We were nine children living in a two-bedroom house. We were living five doors away from a shebeen, which became the headquarters of the local gang in the area.

"I fared pretty well at school. While the other guys were hanging on the street corners, I liked going to school and to the soccer field. I often went to the library and I took other boys with me. I learnt to play chess. I enjoyed the Boy Scouts. It was interesting because it was different, having some form of organised activity. It was different to hanging around and doing nothing or getting involved with other youth who had a bad influence on one. I didn't end up a gangster largely because of that – being in the Scouts, being in a chess club, being in a soccer group while the other guys decided to hang around on the street corners. A good percentage, probably 60 or 70 per cent of them, turned out to be gangsters. Drinking and problems with alcohol and drugs were pretty much part of the way of life for most of these guys.

"When I finished matric, there was no money for studying. The only place where you could get money was the state, but you had to become a teacher or social worker to get a bursary. I went to UWC where I got a bursary and enrolled for social work, later changing my course of studies to do a teachers' diploma. In those days there was no assistance available to become engineers or anything like that. If you came from a poor community, your parents could not finance you. About 80 per cent of the matriculants in my group became teachers or social workers.

"The year 1976 was a big factor in my life. I remember one Sunday evening there was a meeting in the Church of the Resurrection. A guy I only remember as Keith, who was studying theology at UWC at the time, spoke, and I was deeply influenced. It was the time of black consciousness, and he used all the slogans of black consciousness in his speech. He spoke about being black and about being proud to be black. That was the first time I heard that I was black. I had never thought of myself as being black. We had always been coloured. The Africans who stayed in Langa and Gugulethu were black. We grew up with the notion that the milkman was black and we were coloured. It was not a political issue. It was just the way it was. For the first time I became aware of the notion of apartheid and what the National Party had done. I liked the idea of being black as opposed to being white. I was seriously attracted to this idea.

"At that meeting where Keith spoke, we decided to call for a boycott in solidarity with what was happening in Soweto. UWC decided to join the protests and I had my first introduction to teargas, because the police moved in on us and tear-gassed us at school.

"In that week we decided to march to Gugulethu. We felt the black community needed to connect with each other. We had never been there in our lives, although it was within walking distance of our school.

When we got there we didn't know where the schools were, we didn't know a soul there and we didn't know how to ask people where we should be going. We didn't even think of preparing ourselves; it was an extremely spontaneous act. Thousands of students just marched over the bridge, got caught and got beaten up quite badly by the police. We tried to run into people's houses, but we stood out like a sore thumb. Some of the darker students got away, but others were not so lucky.

"There was a student called February who was shot through the eyes with birdshot. I remember a woman being shot next to me. We didn't dare stop. We were scared. We were youngsters and this was the first time that we had experienced brutality in such a direct way."

Trevor spoke about his political activities in the 1980s. "I struggled with the notion of blackness, because I said I was black, but it was never cemented with an experience of black people and black lives. In 1980, we did not really get to know black people, because all these things were happening among us as coloured people. We formed youth organisations and other community organisations, such as the Electricity Petition Campaign in Mitchells Plain. All of this led up to the formation of the United Democratic Front in August 1983.

"The ten years between 1980 and 1990 were dedicated to political organisations. I was president of the Cape Youth Congress [Cayco] when it was launched in 1983. In 1985, I became vice-president when Rose Sonto became president. Life was all about organisations and politics and we pretty much didn't do anything else."

Asked about some of his personal experiences of racism, Trevor said he did not have many to relate. "I had an incident where somebody tried to push me out of a check-out queue in a supermarket, because, for some strange reason, he believed that he should be helped first. I said, 'Do you think because you are white you should be helped first?' I addressed him very directly, and that immediately threw him because he did not know how to respond. He was in an awkward position and I just left it at that.

"That is a cruder form of racism. However, in the workplace I find that white people especially have formed cliques. Whether this is cultural or whether it is racism mixed with culture, I don't know.

"I also see the way senior white staff members at the *Cape Argus* relate to young African journalists and how they would relate to me, for instance. But the difference is that I can assert myself and they know I can. But they are very dismissive of young African journalists. They aren't like that with white people or people they regard as their equals.

"I will normally call the white staff member to one side and immediately address my concerns. I will tell him or her that it is not right to treat people like that."

Naledi Pandor

Grace Naledi Mandisa Pandor is South Africa's Minister of Education and a prominent member of the ANC. She was Chairperson of the National Council of Provinces at the time of the interview.

Naledi was born in Durban in December 1953. Her family lived in a very mixed community. "There were Indians, coloureds, whites and Africans. I started off by going to a coloured school. I don't know how this came about, because on our birth certificates it said we were Bantus.

"After the end of the [1956] Treason Trial in 1960, my father [Joe Samuels, a deputy minister in the first post-apartheid government] was ordered to leave by the ANC. My father and grandfather [Z. K. Matthews, a former ANC president] had both been part of the Treason Trial. We went to Lesotho. It was my first experience of living in a predominantly African community. We also had to learn a new language. Up until that point we had only spoken English and Zulu. Now we also had to learn Sesotho. Finally we moved to England. That was really the first place I could call a settled home. I was ten years old at the time. It was 1964. We first stayed in Hammersmith with lots of South Africans. There were so many people in those flats. Everybody used to come past there: even Mr Mbeki used to visit from time to time.

"We stayed in England for seven years and then my dad was deployed to Botswana. At university in Botswana, I met South Africans for the first time. I was educated by South Africans. Between 1973 and 1976, lots of South Africans came to Botswana."

After graduating in English and History, gaining a bachelor's degree and a Certificate of Education from the University of Botswana and Swaziland in 1977, Naledi continued her education in London, receiving a master's degree in Education from the University of London in 1978. She also obtained a master's in General Linguistics at the University of Stellenbosch in 1997.

"In 1984, I decided I wanted to return to South Africa. I got a job in a rural part of what was then the Bophuthatswana homeland. While I was there, I started to become more involved in the education politics of South Africa. I was impressed by the defiance of the youth. Many people who lived in the cities did not know that, in those days, the South African Defence Force controlled the universities. They would be everywhere. But still the youth organised and remained defiant.

"My husband and I felt that we wanted to put something back into the community, so we formed an evening school for domestic workers and others. The Defence Force felt suspicious about this and decided to patrol around our classrooms every night. Eventually they intimidated the people so much that we had to close the evening school.

"In 1988, while at university, I was centrally involved in launching a non-racial academic organisation called the Union of Democratic Universities of South Africa [UDUSA]." Naledi went on to become a senior lecturer at the University of Cape Town from 1989. She was elected to Parliament as an ANC member following South Africa's first democratic elections in 1994 and became deputy chief whip a year later. Following the June 1999 elections she was elected deputy chairperson of the National Council of Provinces (NCOP) and was chancellor of the Cape Technikon and a member of the council of the University of Fort Hare from 2002 to 2004. She became Minister of Education after the 2004 elections.

I asked her whether she wanted to talk about any of her personal experiences of racism. She related what happened to her at the University of Stellenbosch (an Afrikaans-medium institution) after being nominated onto the university council. She explained that this was not so much a racist incident as it was "cultural and linguistic".

"I am not Afrikaans speaking and have not been able to learn the language. I can understand it a little bit, but I do not understand what they call *suiwer* [pure] Afrikaans.

"I discovered that in the council meetings they only spoke Afrikaans. When they invited me to join the council, they never said anything about meetings being conducted in Afrikaans only. I sat there not knowing what was going on. I did this for a number of months, really just being polite. With hindsight, I think I was being foolish.

"Eventually, I raised my voice about it and the members of council tried once or twice to speak English to accommodate me, but I could see it was an accommodation and they hated having to do it. One day the rector told me that it was their right to speak Afrikaans as a matter of principle. I said I did not want to interfere with their right, but as a council member, I needed to know what was going on. They then said they would provide me with an interpreter.

"They put a woman next to me who would tell me what people said as they spoke. Of course, listening to her made it impossible for me to get all the viewpoints so I became non-functional. I resigned. For the first time ever, I resigned without completing the service period. And it was totally unnecessary, in my view.

"Once I had left the university, they decided to put a simultaneous interpretation system in place. The next person who joined, who was not Afrikaans, would have simultaneous interpretation. Maybe my having gone through an embarrassing experience helped to improve the situation in the future."

Tracy-Lee Rosslind

Tracy-Lee Rosslind was in her final year at Wynberg Girls' High School, a former whites-only school in the Western Cape, when the following interview was conducted in mid-2002. She now works for an events management company. She began by discussing her involvement in Interact, a Rotary-sponsored service club for young people.

"At the beginning of this year, as part of Interact, we took 100 Grade 4 children from Manenberg to Froggy Pond near Simonstown.

We took the kids there basically to show them that there is life outside the crime barriers.

"It was very interesting because a lot of the kids had bruises from beatings. The teachers were actually walking around with sticks to discipline the children. We had to sit down with the teachers and show them that there is another way. The children listened to us and we were not carrying sticks.

"We also put together rape relief boxes because of the high statistics of rape in the Western Cape. We took shoeboxes and packed them with necessities such as face cloths, soaps, deodorants, sanitary towels, underwear and a toy, and we distributed these throughout the police stations. They told us that when the kids came in to report rape cases they didn't have any of these things and some of them came in without any underwear."

Tracy-Lee grew up in Heathfield (a coloured area) before moving to Bergvliet (a former white area) in 1994. I asked her whether she could remember her first day at a white school. "My parents were crying," she said. "I walked into Wynberg Girls' Primary and there were plenty of white faces. Up until this point in time I had been at a coloured school, because schools like Wynberg had been closed to different races. It was in 1991 and I was doing Sub A [Grade One]. It was the very year that the schools were opened to all races. I walked into the school with my parents. We were very active in the ANC and we were not sure about whether I should go to this white school, but we were told that if the opportunity arose, we should take it.

"The first few years were fine and I did not experience much racism. In Sub A I hung out more with the white kids than I did with the coloured children. That all changed after Standard Three [Grade Five]. When we put up our hands in class, the teacher would only answer the questions of the white children or take answers from the white children and she would ignore the coloured children completely, like we were not there. My mother had to come into the school and talk to her about it."

I asked her if high school was a different experience. "It has not changed that much. It has just been covered up better. I can't give names, obviously, because the school would kill me. But there is a coloured teacher on the staff who has been teaching us for the past two years, and this white teacher still does not know her name. We have a coloured head girl and a white deputy. After the coloured girl got sworn in, everybody was saying that she was only head girl because she was coloured. This girl had been in leadership positions since Sub A. She was head girl in primary school and everybody knew she would become head girl in high school. She had leadership qualities. But as soon as she took over, it was said that she was a case of black empowerment.

"We went for a talk at UCT and someone told us that blacks would get work first, then the coloureds and then the whites. So whites would never get work. Yet it does not work that way. Yes, there are quotas and there should be, because the fact is that white people are still running things. Now the white people say that it is apartheid in reverse, but if you don't equalise things and give people the same education, then it is never going to work out in the end. The children make comments like, 'We are all going to pass our exams because they have been brought down to the same level as the exams written by the black kids.'

"There is lots of conflict between the coloured and the black children. Coloureds have this mentality that black is wrong and white is right. I find the coloured children are more racist than the white children and the black children, who seem to get on better. The coloureds are in the middle all by themselves. They don't really mix.

"Making fun of people's accents is a major problem at school, as far as I am concerned. At our school it is looked upon as a joke. The white people make fun of the coloured people's accents even in class. Some of the coloured people even laugh at this, because they think it is a joke, but it is not a joke. They are making fun of who you are, your culture and your people. How can it be regarded as a joke? They say I have this colour phobia and I must stop being like that.

"There was once a race argument in class when I was absent. The teacher even said, 'Thank goodness Tracy-Lee wasn't here otherwise it would have been another lecture.' The teachers are not teaching the children what is happening in the world, so sometimes I feel I have to."

I asked Tracy-Lee about her ANC background. "As long as I can remember, my family has been ANC. My whole family, including my grandparents, is ANC. We have always been pro-black, pro-ANC and pro-new South Africa. I can still remember being kitted out in my ANC gear and going to Hout Bay for rallies. I remember meeting Nelson Mandela when we had a function for him, and I remember that my father still kissed the pen after Mandela had signed with it. We had lots of leaders come to our home when we lived in Heathfield, such as Trevor Manuel. Those people were my role models.

"That is why I am so passionate about the whole racial thing. People have forgotten, but my parents went through all these things. Now we have a new government, but we cannot forget the past."

Keathelia Satto

Keathelia Satto, a learner at a former white Afrikaans school in the Western Cape, described herself as coloured. When I interviewed her in 2002 she was in Grade Eight.

"My entire schooling has been Model C," she said. "When I went to Excelsior, most of the children were white, and there were only a few coloureds. The whites did not bother too much with me, but the coloured children used to make fun of me because I was so dark. A girl came up to me once and asked me why I wore black clothes. She said, 'Why don't you take off that black top? You are already black.' Coloureds can be racist towards other coloureds."

She said that the situation at high school was a bit different. "People do not insult me that much any more, but they often do it without knowing they are doing it. Most of the children at my high school are coloured. It has changed over the last year or so, with more coloureds coming to the school."

I asked her how the white children, at what used to be an Afrikaner school, were coping. "The whites who are there want to be like coloureds. They even try to speak like coloureds."

Keathelia did not feel that attending a mixed-race school meant she was better equipped to deal with issues around racism than children who went to "coloureds-only" schools. "I have a friend who goes to

Malibu High [a coloureds-only school] and I think they are better off than us. They are dealing with stuff in the community and they don't have racism and stuff like that in their school. Most of those children have been together since primary school."

However, she agreed that the quality of education she was getting at a former white school was probably better than what she would have received at a black school. There were 25 children in her class. Most of the black schools had at least 40 and sometimes even more than 50 children per class. The teachers at her school were mainly white. She said she found this strange, given the number of coloured children at her school, but that they did have a few coloured teachers. "The children relate to the coloured teachers in the same way as they relate to the white teachers," she said.

There were five white children in Keathelia's class, and a few Africans. I asked her how she related to the African children. "They are in my class, but I don't communicate too much with them. They are always in their own clique. I don't know why. I only have coloured friends," she said.

I asked her whether the coloured children also formed their own cliques. "Yes, they do, but there is not even a white clique at my school. The whites are almost like coloureds so they mix with the coloureds." She explained what she meant by white people trying to be like coloured people. "There is this boy who lives in Plattekloof. He is white, but he is coloured in the way that he talks and he just hangs out with coloured people. I have a friend who is half white, half coloured. Her father is white, but he does not live with them any more. She always defends coloureds. She looks like a white person, but she is half-coloured."

Did she believe that all schools in the future should have a majority of African or coloured children and a minority of white children? "I think it should be equal. I don't think there should be more whites or more blacks. It should be equal."

I asked her whether she found it difficult or easy to make friends with whites. "It is difficult because whites don't know your background, so you won't be able to communicate with them at first. If you make friends with a coloured, you will be able to talk about your area and stuff like that."

Athena and Manny Sotomi

Athena Sotomi was born and grew up in District Six. After her family was removed from District Six, she lived in Belgravia Estate on the Cape Flats. "I then moved to England and lived there for three years, before returning to South Africa."

Athena attended the Holy Cross Convent School in District Six and Immaculata High School. She did not go to university but studied journalism at the London School of Publishing and at the Cape Technikon in Cape Town. She wrote for newspapers while she was in London, but had not written for three years at the time of the interview in February 2002.

Manny Sotomi said his story was "a little bit more complicated" than Athena's. "I was born in Lagos, Nigeria, but I grew up in Britain and America. I served some time as an officer in the British Army. I worked in Britain for a few years. I married Athena after I met her in London."

Manny said his father was a general in the British Army and "my mother was a jack of all trades, sometimes housekeeper, sometimes journalist, sometimes this, sometimes that, and foremost a mother". Manny went to Thornton School in Somerset, an English public school. He did his first degree at Anglo University and his second degree at Oxford University. He was with the British Army until their barracks got shut down. He worked for several corporations as a planning adviser. "After I met Athena, we came to South Africa to have a baby, and I stayed."

I asked Manny to relate some of his personal experiences of racism. "When my brother was here a few years ago, I went with him and his white American girlfriend, Jackie, to a night club in Camps Bay. This truck came along and blocked us off. There were three burly white men in the truck.

"Jackie started to cry. They were speaking Afrikaans and asked us what we were doing with a white girl. My father was a soldier and I was a soldier; I don't know how to back off from confrontation. My brother is the same. So I jumped out of the car. One of them made the mistake of getting out of his car. I grabbed hold of him and the other two reversed and drove off. The one who remained behind was literally in tears. He said it was not fair, because now there were two of us. My brother told me to get back in the car and said to this guy, 'Now it is fair, just me against you.'

"Then I saw a bunch of bastards sprinting towards us, so my brother and I both stood our ground and told these guys, 'Let's go.' When they saw we were not budging and Jackie was crying and speaking in an American accent, they kind of eased off. Then they invited us to have a drink with them. I told them to get lost. The fact of the matter is that racists are cowards.

"There are so many stories to tell. Once, when we lived in Woodstock [in Cape Town], I went to go buy wood. I was driving a huge BMW 730 at the time. I parked in front of the shop and got out of the car. There was a bunch of young white men sitting on the corner. I took two bags of wood. I paid and was about to take the bags of wood to my car when this young black kid came along and asked whether he could help me carry them. He obviously wanted a tip. I said 'okay'.

"He was struggling to pick up the one bag and one of the white young men said something about a 'Kaffir'. I was new in town and knew that 'Kaffir' was something like 'nigger'.

"I turned around, walked up to the white man and asked him what he had said. He said he was not speaking to me. Before I knew it, reflex took over and I floored him. I warned the rest of them that I would kill him if they did not back off. I think they were shocked.

"I walked to the car and opened the boot. The young black kid put the wood in the car, I gave him R2 and he started running. I then realised that I had messed up that kid's deal. He helped people at that shop, but now he could not go back there, because those white guys were going to beat the hell out of him. I felt that I had taken an opportunity away from him."

Athena related a story about the day they had caught a thief inside their BMW. "This guy, we later learnt, was from Manenberg. He was sitting in the car with the tape deck on his lap," she said. "Manny knocked on the window and asked him what he was doing and it took the thief a few seconds to realise that this black man was actually the owner of this car. He opened the front door and ran off."

Manny continued the story: "I gave chase and did something very rash. I tackled him on the tarmac. The police were very good. They arrived very quickly. That in itself was very dramatic for me, because of the history and reputation of the police under apartheid in South Africa. Here was this young black kid, I had tackled him and was handing him over to the police. That was a major dilemma for me. I felt that I should let him go."

"But he did not want to let go of the tape recorder," said Athena.

Manny added: "Yes, and I realised that the car was not insured and that he could have had a gun and shot me or shot other people. I made a decision to hand him over to the police and to go and testify in court against him. He eventually ended up in jail. Hopefully he learnt his lesson and came out of jail a better person."

Athena said that the way she dealt with racist individuals was to consider racism the other person's problem and not hers. She related the following story. "My mother and I were in a factory shop. We were looking at some stuff and this older Afrikaans woman asked my mother something and called her a *meid*."

Manny asked her what *meid* meant and Athena explained, "It is a derogatory term for a coloured woman. It is like calling a person a washerwoman. This woman was trying to start a conversation and used the term in what she considered a harmless way. I just lost it and said, 'Who the hell do you think you are talking to?' That really made me angry. She backed off and she said she was sorry.

"This experience has really stuck in my mind and will stay with me, because it was just too much for me. But you get black people also being racist. It is not just white against black."

Melanie Verwoerd
Melanie Verwoerd was the youngest elected female Member of Parliament and the former South African ambassador to Ireland, where she now lives. She is married to Wilhelm, the grandson of the architect of apartheid, Hendrick Verwoerd. She currently presents Spectrum on RTE Radio 1, a show that highlights issues of diversity and multiculturalism.

When I interviewed her in early 2002, she said that she had grown up like most white Afrikaner children. "I was born in Pretoria, but grew up mostly in Stellenbosch. Like everyone else in Stellenbosch, I went to a white school and a white church, and I lived in a white neighbourhood.

"I did a very funny thing when I went to university. I studied theology in the Dutch Reformed Church. I really wanted to be a minister, even though women could not be ordained at that stage. I was the only woman in a class of 40 men. I studied theology for three years. In my third year, the Dutch Reformed Church Synod decided to allow women to become ordained. They also had to decide whether they were going to allow all races. My reading of the situation at the time was that it was easier to ordain women than to deal with the issue of race. I was very disillusioned and angry about the issues in the church.

"In my second and third year, things started to change for me politically. Wilhelm left to take up his Rhodes scholarship in the middle of 1986. He first spent some time in Holland and ended up in a house with ANC exiles. I became involved in Idasa [the Institute for Democracy in South Africa] and the National Union of South African Students. Wilhelm started sending me some banned books, so I began reading things that I could not get in South Africa at the time.

"At the end of 1986 I went to visit him at Oxford and we met up with South African exiles in London. They told us about a country that I did not know of, and I will be forever thankful for that. Wilhelm and I got married and I completed my honour's degree in Philosophy. I then started doing an MA in Feminist Theology. That was in 1988. During that time, while we were at Oxford, the ANC was unbanned and we returned to South Africa in 1990 with a small baby.

"When I returned to South Africa, it was very difficult. I came back to a country that had completely changed, in my view. I could no longer trust every single authority that I had trusted up to that point. I realised that they had all lied and colluded with apartheid.

"Part of me wanted to join the ANC immediately, but we were also mindful that many whites who came back from overseas were joining the ANC on the rebound. We wanted to make sure that we were not doing that. Also, we were conscious of Wilhelm's family and the problems our membership of the ANC would cause for them.

"Towards the end of 1990 we met President Mandela at a cocktail function at Stellenbosch and we had a long chat with him. Wilhelm told him that he wanted to apologise and we had a lovely and significant discussion. I joined the ANC shortly after that.

I asked Melanie to tell me about her parents. "I think they both supported the National Party in the past. I learnt a lot from my mother, not in a political sense, but more in a social sense. We would take clothes to the poor people and that kind of thing. We did a lot of charity work, but there was no political context at all. We were not that politicised, even though my father did work for the National Party.

"When we joined the ANC, it obviously caused a lot of upset in my family, especially my extended family. My grandparents were very upset."

Melanie said it helped that she had never been a member of the National Party. "It was far more complicated for Wilhelm because he had been part of the Ruyterwacht, the Junior Broederbond. Also because of where he came from, when you have a surname that is so visible in the Afrikaner community and you have to look up daily at huge pictures of your grandfather, it certainly becomes more complicated. It was very difficult for him."

Melanie said that she must have had personal experiences of racism. "But I cannot recall any of them," she said. "Even in the ANC, in the beginning, people expected certain things and assumed certain things about me. But we have also had situations where we were sitting in a meeting and people would talk about whites and the Boere and they would apologise to me. That annoyed me. It was far more amazing when people would say that they didn't see me as a white any more."

Obed Zilwa and Leo de Souza
Leo de Souza was the communications manager for the mayor of Cape Town at the time of the interview. She still works for the city.

Leo was born in Springs, Gauteng, to an Afrikaans mother and a Portuguese father. "We moved to a mining town called Secunda, in

Mpumalanga. It was a very small town," she said. "My mother is Afrikaans. Her name was Louise Louw. My father, Louis de Souza, is Portuguese. He is from Madeira in Portugal. I have two brothers. We were a very average family, who lived in a middle-class mining town. It was a very secure and protected environment.

"I was never part of the struggle and I never claim to have been. I remember being at Tukkies [the University of Pretoria], which was a very Afrikaans university, when a whole bunch of students from Wits [the University of the Witwatersrand] came to demonstrate. I remember walking past them and telling them to get a life.

"After completing my three-year drama degree, I went to Gauteng and started doing some public relations work. I also got involved in a little bit of journalism. When I went back to Secunda I started working at the local newspaper, called *The Echo*. I met up with a guy called Mohammed Bhabha, who later became a senator and served in the National Council of Provinces. He was an anti-apartheid lawyer at the time and he introduced me to what was happening. This was in the late 1980s or early 1990s. He made me politically aware and re-educated me on many levels.

"I was very fortunate that I met Nelson Mandela about two or three months after he was released. I started doing some work with the ANC, just minor PR stuff. After the election I went to Gauteng and I decided that I was going to leave journalism and go into PR.

"I can't remember applying for a job in government, but I remember getting a call one day and the person told me they were going to write the Constitution and that I had been shortlisted for an interview as the PR manager for the Constitutional Assembly. I went to Cape Town for the interview, convinced that I was just making up the numbers, but two weeks later they called me and told me I had the job.

"After that I met Obed and I am not leaving Cape Town again. I am staying."

Obed Zilwa is a photographer for Associated Press. He was born in Nyanga in Cape Town. "In 1985, my dad was involved in a strike. I left school because my mother could not cope. My dad was working on his own. My mother never worked, apart from selling bread, *vetkoek* and *frikkadels* to keep us going. So I decided to help her," he said.

"It was during those days that the struggle started getting heavy and many people were getting killed. Almost every weekend there was a funeral in the township. One day I was walking and I saw this man with a bald head carrying a camera. His name was Alf Khumalo. He was with Peter Magubane and John Rubython [famous South African photographers]. I was walking next to them with a little camera. At that time, I was already taking pictures, but I did not really see myself as a photographer, as much as I liked photography. I was taking pictures of parties and girls at school.

"I heard them say they were thirsty because it was very hot. Without asking them whether they wanted water, I ran across the road in NY6 and got a jug of water. I gave the water to John, who gave it to Peter. John then gave me his business card. That was the Saturday. The Sunday I went to visit his studio and that was when I decided that I was finished with school.

"I started taking pictures. I became a fixer, driving them around, finding a way for them to get into the township and driving their cars with no licence. One day I went to John's studio and he had left a note on the door saying: 'Go back home and get dressed nicely. Go to the *Cape Times* to meet a man called Chris Greyvenstein.' I went there to meet this man and the next thing I was told to start. That was how I started out in photography and I am still doing it today."

In April 2000, Obed was arrested in Zimbabwe on suspicion of involvement in a bomb that exploded near a hotel where many foreign journalists were staying. He was released after protests from journalists, human rights organisations and governments throughout the world.

I asked the couple how they had met. "I had just bought myself a video camera and I used to go to Manenberg's Jazz Café all the time because I love to take pictures of jazz musicians," said Obed. "One day I saw this person and I kept on taking pictures of her. She basically told me to 'eff off'. Later I went to her and introduced myself. She told me she was a PR for the Constitutional Assembly and we exchanged cards."

Leo took over the story: "I was at Manenberg's all the time. It was a good place just to drink and enjoy oneself. One day, I got very drunk and Obed took me home. Before he took me home, like a true gentleman, he took me to a place where they served me a cocktail that made me sober. That was about six years ago, in 1996."

Obed related an incident that happened at Cape Town's V&A Waterfront. "It was in December and the Waterfront was very busy. I saw this lady crying in her car and her children were also crying. She was struggling with a man. I decided to investigate.

"The man, who was the lady's husband, wanted to take her cheque book and had already broken the front windscreen. I said I would call the police and he called me a Kaffir. He was from Johannesburg and Afrikaans-speaking. She said I should not intervene because he was going to hit me. I thought I must call the police, before he decided to kill everyone. He started hitting me and I gave him a couple of smacks. Eventually the police came, calmed him down and put him in the police van.

"This man was this woman's husband and obviously the fact that he called me a Kaffir probably means that they discuss these kinds of things at home. But as I was leaving, she called me her darling for saving her. It shows that people can change. Something can happen to make them change."

My thoughts

As I mentioned in the introduction, part of my aim in writing this book was to refute some of the racial stereotypes that exist. Nevertheless, the perceptions formed while growing up create a lasting impression in one's mind. And the notion that I had in my mind as a young person was that whites were normally the bosses, Indians were normally shopkeepers, coloureds were working class and Africans were below coloureds.

There are two incidents that stand out in my memory, which helped me to confront these preconceptions. The first occurred when I travelled overseas for the first time, while there was still apartheid in South Africa. I arrived at Heathrow Airport, went into the bathroom, and discovered a white man cleaning the toilet. I almost wanted to offer to help him clean it, because this did not fit the image of the white man that I had in my mind.

The other incident occurred when we moved to Durban in 1993, and for the first time I saw Indian men working on the garbage trucks that collected our dirt in the mornings. Again, this did not match my idea of Indians.

The above mentioned incidents assisted me in dealing with my inner racist by disputing some of my preconceptions. In conducting the interviews, I found that my notions of race were further challenged by some of the unexpected attitudes and responses of the interviewees, confirming what I had suspected: that there is no clear-cut, easy definition of racism, and no neat South African identity – topics I explore in the following two chapters.

Chapter 2
Who are we?

Is there such a thing as a South African identity?

The dilemma of being coloured

In the 1980s, it was easy to identify when people were talking about coloured people. They would raise both their hands to about face height, extend their middle and index fingers and move them up and down to make quotation marks or "air quotes", an indication that they were talking about "so-called" coloured people. Nowadays, the quotation marks have disappeared and people just talk about coloured people. No more so-called.

But where does this leave people who may or may not look like coloured people but do not necessarily want to be associated with being a coloured? And what does it mean to look like a coloured?

I have never been able to relate to being a coloured, because I struggle to understand on what basis one becomes a coloured. Is it because of skin colour? It cannot be, because some coloureds are whiter than most whites, while other coloureds are blacker than most Africans.

Is it because of hair texture? I don't think so, because some coloureds have the straightest and shiniest hair, while others have hair that is so curly that they would never have passed the old apartheid-era pencil test, where government officials would stick a pencil into a person's hair to determine his or her race. If the pencil stuck, then that person would be considered black. If the pencil fell out, then that person could be declared white.

Is it because of culture? Again, it cannot be. In terms of music, some coloureds believe in the culture of the Cape Coon (or Minstrel) Carnivals or the Cape Malay Choirs, while others reject this. Some coloureds feel more comfortable with African music, while others feel more comfortable with American music. A few even like classical music, while many grew up in the church choir tradition. In terms of food, people classified as coloureds have varied tastes, from curries traditionally associated with Indians to samp and beans normally associated with Africans. In terms of religion, some coloureds are Christians while others are Muslim, and many are associated with other religions or with no religion at all.

Is it because of language? No, coloureds speak different languages. There are those (mainly in the Cape) who speak Afrikaans, while some (especially those from Durban) cannot even speak Afrikaans and only speak English. Others, especially those from Gauteng or KwaZulu-Natal, are comfortable speaking African languages such as Zulu, Xhosa or Sotho.

Or is it simply a way of defining people who cannot be defined in any other way?

I have always believed that the last reason is probably the most likely. I believe that the apartheid government created a category of people and called them coloureds, because they had no other way of defining them. But even if they did not create this category, they certainly perpetuated it in a negative way, to their advantage. This was in line with the policy of divide and rule. It was not in their interest for Africans, coloureds and Indians alike to consider themselves black. It was in their interest to splinter these groups into Africans, Coloureds and Indians, and to split them further into Cape Coloureds, Other Coloureds, Cape Malays, Xhosas, Zulus, Sothos, Tswanas, Tamils, Hindus, and so on. This was why the ideas of Steve Biko were so refreshing. By referring to ourselves as black, it meant that we opposed the apartheid government's definitions of ourselves.

Throughout the seventies and eighties, I was accepted by the majority of South Africans as a black South African. In the nineties, however, after we had won our freedom, I noticed a disturbing trend. Among those people who used to accept me as black, I was now only a coloured. I had gone from being part of the majority to being part of the minority.

Part of the reason for this, I believe, is economic. For many years, coloureds in South Africa had special privileges under apartheid. For instance, the Western Cape was considered a coloured labour preference area. That meant that if you started a business in the Western Cape, you would have to employ only coloured workers. African workers had to apply for special permits or passes to be allowed into the Western Cape.

Coloured people also had access to better social and welfare services than Africans in the Western Cape. Part of the government's divide and rule strategy was based on the homeland system, which meant that Africans had so-called self-rule in homelands, which were normally far away from the industrial heartlands of South Africa. These homelands were normally in semi-rural or rural areas, and had no real prospect of offering jobs to the people who lived there. As a result, many Africans had to travel to the cities to look for jobs. Because they needed permits and passes to be in the cities, many African men went to these cities by themselves and left their wives in the homelands.

Now that the economic pie is open to all, there is a logical sense among some Africans that coloureds and Indians should be excluded from acquiring wealth, because they were not as oppressed under apartheid as Africans were. Their feeling is that the fewer people who benefit from the new economic pie, the more there will be for everyone in this smaller group to share.

There is also a sense that the majority of people classified as coloured feel more comfortable interacting with whites than they do with Africans. This is seen as one of the reasons why the African National Congress failed to win the Western Cape in the last two elections. Coloured people supposedly felt threatened by Africans, because they did not know what to expect from African rule, and voted for the whites based on this fear. In Trevor Oosterwyk's words, it was a case of "better the devil you know than the one you don't know".

Grappling with identity

Not only coloureds are grappling with their identities in South Africa today; most South Africans are still struggling to find an appropriate way to describe themselves. In the old days, we used to call black people "Africans", because during apartheid South Africa was cut off from the rest of the continent. However, now that South Africa has taken its rightful place on the African continent, all South Africans, including whites, want to be called Africans. This is despite the fact, I must note, that many English-speaking whites still hold onto British passports, while claiming their African heritage.

Black is a term that has historically been used to describe people who are not white, and which includes coloureds and Indians. It is not politically correct to identify people by tribal names such as Xhosa, Zulu or Sotho. While these groups existed way before apartheid, the apartheid government tried to pronounce these tribal differences in a way that would benefit their divide-and-rule strategy. The apartheid government also used terms such as "non-whites", "non-Europeans", "natives", "Bantu" and "plurals" to describe the black majority. At some point, the apartheid government referred to whites as European. This was until someone pointed out to them that there were many black people who came from Europe.

Indian people have also grappled with their identity. Yes, they are descendants of people who came from India originally, but is it appropriate to call them "Indians" when many of them have been in South Africa for generations and might never even visit India? And what about other people of Asian descent?

For the sake of consistency, and to keep in line with the official norm in South Africa, I will use the term "black" to refer to everyone who is not white, including Africans, coloureds and Indians. I will use the term "African" to describe people who would otherwise be called black, and I will use the terms "coloureds", "Indians" and "whites" to describe South Africa's other major race groups. Where I need to refer to other groups, for instance Chinese, I will refer to them as such.

The need for a new race language

It is clear that there is a need for a new language to describe different groups in South Africa. The existing terminology is too loaded with apartheid-era baggage. It is also confusing, especially for foreigners who visit our country, but even for South Africans.

When one reads about black people in the newspapers, for instance, one has to read carefully to discern whether blacks are being referred to generically, or specifically as Africans. A term such as "African" is also problematic because, rightly, all people born in South Africa or anywhere else on the continent are entitled to call themselves "African".

The Americans have dealt with their identity issues by adding a prefix to the word "American". Therefore they refer to African-Americans, Chinese-Americans, Italian-Americans or Spanish-Americans, to indicate people's country of origin. This would not necessarily work in South Africa, where many South Africans have an unclear ancestry going back hundreds of years and where racial classification has been based on factors other than geographic origin.

There are some people in South Africa who have begun to use terms such as "coloured black", "Indian black" and "African black". However, the people who are using these terms are but a small minority in South Africa and I don't know whether this custom will ever take off.

There are various opinions and suggestions that have been put forward, but I believe what is important is that South Africans start engaging each other on the issue of identity.

Thabo Mbeki: I am an African

South African president, Thabo Mbeki (then deputy president), made his famous "I am an African" speech in Cape Town on 8 May 1996, on behalf of the ruling ANC on the occasion of the adoption by the Constitutional Assembly of the Republic of South Africa Constitution Bill 1996.

In one of the most poetic speeches ever made by a leader anywhere in the world, he declared:

I am an African.

I owe my being to the hills and the valleys, the mountains and the glades, the rivers, the deserts, the trees, the flowers, the seas and the ever-changing seasons that define the face of our native land.

My body has frozen in our frosts and in our latter day snows. It has thawed in the warmth of our sunshine and melted in the heat of the midday sun. The crack and the rumble of the summer thunders, lashed by startling lightning, have been a cause both of trembling and of hope.

The fragrances of nature have been as pleasant to us as the sight of the wild blooms of the citizens of the veld.

The dramatic shapes of the Drakensberg, the soil-coloured waters of the Lekoa, iGqili noThukela, and the sands of the Kgalagadi, have all been panels of the set on the natural stage on which we act out the foolish deeds of the theatre of our day.

At times, and in fear, I have wondered whether I should concede equal citizenship of our country to the leopard and the lion, the elephant and the springbok, the hyaena, the black mamba and the pestilential mosquito.

A human presence among all these, a feature on the face of our native land thus defined, I know that none dare challenge me when I say – I am an African!

I owe my being to the Khoi and the San whose desolate souls haunt the great expanses of the beautiful Cape – they who fell victim to the most merciless genocide our native land has ever seen, they who were the first to lose their lives in the struggle to defend our freedom and dependence and they who, as a people, perished in the result.

Today, as a country, we keep an audible silence about these ancestors of the generations that live, fearful to admit the horror of a former deed, seeking to obliterate from our memories a cruel occurrence which, in its remembering, should teach us not and never to be inhuman again.

I am formed of the migrants who left Europe to find a new home on our native land. Whatever their own actions, they remain still, part of me.

In my veins courses the blood of the Malay slaves who came from the East. Their proud dignity informs my bearing, their culture a part of my essence. The stripes they bore on their bodies from the lash of the slave master are a reminder embossed on my consciousness of what should not be done.

I am the grandchild of the warrior men and women that Hintsa and Sekhukhune led, the patriots that Cetshwayo and Mphephu took to battle, the soldiers Moshoeshoe and Ngungunyane taught never to dishonour the cause of freedom.

My mind and my knowledge of myself are formed by the victories that are the jewels in our African crown, the victories we earned from Isandhlwana to Khartoum, as Ethiopians and as the Ashanti of Ghana, as the Berbers of the desert.

I am the grandchild who lays fresh flowers on the Boer graves at St Helena and the Bahamas, who sees in the mind's eye and suffers the suffering of a simple peasant folk, death, concentration camps, destroyed homesteads, a dream in ruins.

I am the child of Nongqause. I am he who made it possible to trade in the world markets in diamonds, in gold, in the same food for which my stomach yearns.

I come of those who were transported from India and China, whose being resided in the fact, solely, that they were able to provide physical labour, who taught me that we could both be at home and be foreign, who taught me that human existence itself demanded that freedom was a necessary condition for that human existence.

Being part of all these people, and in the knowledge that none dare contest that assertion, I shall claim that – I am an African.

This speech was widely quoted by several of the speakers at a conference on race and identity hosted by the Cape Town-based Institute for Justice and Reconciliation (IJR) in December 2001.

No one pointed out the major flaw in this speech, however: Mbeki, despite all his fantastic poetry, failed to deal with the central issue of what it means to be a South African as opposed to an African. He also did not deal with the key issue of racial classification. Although it could be assumed that his speech was alluding to a blurring of separate identities or that he was in fact describing a South African and not a broader African identity, he still falls short of the key question: What do we do about existing categories or descriptions of people in South Africa today? A criticism of the Mbeki presidency from opposition quarters, rightly or wrongly, has been that he is able to deal with global and African issues in a very accomplished manner, but he is not entirely comfortable with South African issues.

I tried to probe this question – what it means to be a South African – during my interviews, and asked several questions to determine how my interviewees related to identity in South Africa. Among the questions were: "How do you describe yourself?", "Does your description of yourself differ from the way other people describe you?", "What is the most derogatory description that you have had to endure?", "Do you think your background has affected the way people relate to you in society?" and "How does one remain true to one's identity without being racist?" What follows are excerpts from their responses, in no particular order.

Phatekile Holomisa

Asked to describe himself, Phatekile initially answered: "I do not describe myself."

He then explained that there was always conflict between what factor was more important than another in terms of descriptions of oneself. "I am first of all Phatekile Holomisa, the son of Mathatisa, and leader of the AmaHegebe clan, a Thembu. But, of course, I am also a South African, so I am all of those things. I am a politician and a member of the ANC. I am a Member of Parliament and I am also a traditional leader. I am a Xhosa-speaking South African, but I also speak English."

Asked how other people described him, he said that most people would call him by his clan name or by his traditional name.

I asked him if he had ever had to endure derogatory descriptions of himself. He replied that because of his light complexion, the children he grew up with had called him *ilawu*, which is the Xhosa term for coloured, or *umlungu*, which means white. "However, this was all in playfulness," he said.

Phatekile felt that his background had influenced the way people related to him in society. "Those who know me and know anything about African culture know me as a traditional leader and respect me for that. However, some people also respect the fact that I am a public representative and an advocate. Education also counts. People think that because one is an advocate, one is very important. However, I consider myself to be a very ordinary person. Some of the positions I hold I have acquired. Others, particularly the traditional ones, I did not have a choice in accepting."

Phatekile believed that one remained true to one's identity through education and respect. "You don't need to have an attitude towards other people. You need to accept them for what they are. Like I said, there were some things imposed on me and I had no choice. I understand that other people also did not choose to be who they are. I know that there is no one superior to me, just as I am not superior to anyone.

"It is important to know who you are, and this will help you relate to other people with respect."

Carel Boshoff

Carel Boshoff described himself as an activist. "Sometimes I think of myself for practical reasons as a writer or a journalist. I do some freelance writing for magazines and newspapers and I do some work for the Afrikaans television channel. But if I had to put an umbrella over all of this, then I would say that I am an activist.

"I could have become an academic. I don't know why this did not happen, but I suppose it had to do with decisions one takes at certain times in one's life. Instead I became involved in what one could describe as a movement, which involved a certain way of viewing life and thinking."

I was surprised by this answer. I thought that Carel would have been more likely than anyone else I had interviewed to describe himself in racial terms first.

I asked him how he would describe himself from a racial and cultural perspective. "The definitions of culture and identity in South Africa all carry a heavy burden. It is very difficult to find one word to describe oneself from a cultural identity perspective in South Africa and with which one would feel comfortable.

"I grew up as an Afrikaner and this word had a particular meaning in a particular context. It meant, widely, people who were white or of European descent, who spoke Afrikaans and who belonged to the Christian Protestant religion. This three-point definition was accepted by everyone. I realised later in life that this definition left out one important point, and that is the middle class. I think most white, Afrikaans-speaking Protestants were middle class. This point was never emphasised to gain maximum impact.

"I have also realised that all of this is changing and there is very little left of what used to describe an Afrikaner. The key is still language and therefore it is easier for me to identify myself by an adjective and that is 'Afrikaans'. I think it is also important to look at one's history and I share my history with a group of people who would be called Afrikaners. Some people are outspoken about this, others are not.

"At this point I identify very strongly with what is becoming known as the new Afrikaans movement. There is a movement away from defining Afrikaners in terms of race and associating them instead with an idea, a direction, a confirmation of certain values and meanings."

Asked what his views were on "brown Afrikaners" or coloured people who spoke Afrikaans, Carel said this was a difficult question. "I realise that there are people who define the term 'Afrikaner' very narrowly and exclude coloured people. They say coloureds and whites cannot be part of the same community. I believe we can almost have a federal situation with regards to Afrikaners, with different groups of people making up this broad Afrikaner community, each one having his own identification markers.

"I am comfortable with the idea that Afrikaners do not necessarily have to be an exclusively white concept. However, I am also very realistic about the challenges this poses to a group to redefine themselves and to create a new relationship with other groups who were not part of your community previously.

"I don't know what the outcome will be, because there are all kinds of political powers putting pressure on the situation. For instance, in the past, an association with Afrikaners would have meant easier access to resources, but it no longer means the same thing."

Asked whether his description of himself differed from the way other people described him, he replied: "To my experience, it does. There has been a lot of prejudice in people's judgements of me. I am not complaining, but I must admit that sometimes I struggle to communicate myself properly, to convince people that what they expect from me is not what they will necessarily get.

"I live in Orania, which is a settlement of Afrikaners and it is often portrayed as being a racist concept. But that is not how I see Orania or my involvement in Orania. There are many positive aspects to Orania that people on the outside are not aware of."

He said that he'd never paid much attention to derogatory descriptions of himself: "Whatever comments have been made, I don't think they were related to racism or identity."

Carel said that his background affected the way people related to him in society in a positive and a negative way. "It is difficult to be a white Afrikaner in South Africa today. One has had certain privileges in terms of education and opportunities that were almost exclusive to the Afrikaner. However, one realises nowadays that one is no longer part of the privileged group and that there is a certain level of marginalisation. I don't complain about that. The access to power for different groups changes as history changes and I find it comfortable to be in the position that I am now with regards to that access to power. It is different to the seventies and eighties when access to power was morally indefensible."

Rhoda Kadalie

Human rights activist Rhoda Kadalie said that her political consciousness developed "in a home where we were subjected to the Group Areas Act".

"My parents were removed out of Mowbray quite forcibly. I studied anthropology at the University of the Western Cape and my political awareness grew out of this, because anthropology is the discipline that reflects on social structures, cultures, diversity, racism, how people are created by their society and how society creates their cultures.

"I always rejected the notion of being coloured and embraced the slogan of non-racialism quite easily. But in the post-apartheid South Africa I am quite politically disillusioned around race, because I am being told by the ruling party, in various ways, once again, that I am coloured.

"Now I celebrate my marginality, because one can be what one wants to be in a racially divided landscape. One can appropriate the right to be whatever one wants to be and not subscribe to the racial labels that are forced upon us in a society that is racist."

Asked if her description of herself differed from the way other people described her, Rhoda replied, "Oh yes. For example, I was once asked to participate in a British Broadcasting Corporation [BBC] debate with [Gauteng Premier] Sam Shilowa and [Constitutional Court Judge] Albie Sachs and somebody else whose name I forget. I asked the BBC how they got to hear of me and they said they were looking for an opinionated, cocky, arrogant, black South African and the people said 'Rhoda Kadalie'. I found that very interesting.

Rhoda said she has not had to deal with any offensive descriptions of herself. "However, I think that in their own groups, people do derogatory stuff among each other. We would always joke and deride each other. I don't think it is easy for outsiders to do this."

She said it was clear, in certain circles at least, that her background as a Kadalie influenced the way people related to her. "I am amazed how many people know the history of Clements Kadalie. Even [former South African Education Minister] Kader Asmal, when he returned from exile, said to me, 'You know the history of this great Clements

Kadalie?' He assumed that I probably could not be related purely because I was coloured. So I said, 'Yes, I am his granddaughter' and Kader just laughed. I told him, 'Kader, you know you are behaving like that because your assumption is that Clements was an African Malawian, and therefore because I am coloured we can't be related.' Kader burst out laughing, in acknowledgment that he was wrong.

"When I tell people I am Clements Kadalie's direct granddaughter, they say that, politically, I am a chip off the old block. Not racially, but politically. I find that interesting."

Rhoda said that the struggle for identity could be a very positive experience. "What shapes one's identity is your historical and your social experiences, and that can be positive. When I studied in Holland, we had a cultural evening once a month. The institute where I studied had mostly Third World students from all over the world. I must admit I felt sad because of my lack of patriotism. I had no culture to celebrate. My colleagues came in their national dress, brought food and music, and I had very little to share with them. I think that is because I was denied an identity that I badly wanted. There was nothing I could be proud of as a South African.

"After 1994, coloured people could finally say to Mandela and Thabo Mbeki: 'Doctor Abdurahman, Cissy Gool and Benny Kies were all part of my history.' I find that in the new South Africa those identities are negated. At an election rally in District Six in 1999, it was the first time that Thabo Mbeki mentioned the names of all those people.

"If we had a politically inclusive resistance history, it would make a world of difference to the positive assertion of who we are as a people. People always have to be embarrassed about their colour today, and it is not good for people to feel embarrassed or negative about who they are.

"Zimitri Erasmus wrote this book on identity and race, in which she said that the new South Africa should teach people to live comfortably in their skin. I think that many of us are still not comfortable about who we are. There is a constant quest among coloured people to establish their identity and to understand why they are once again being marginalised.

"If you read the first chapter of Patricia de Lille's book, it is about her roots and is a positive assertion about where she comes from. [De Lille is the leader of the Independent Democrats]. Coloured people always brag about their white ancestry and do not talk about their black ancestry, because they were made to feel embarrassed about it. We need a resurrection of a political, social and cultural history which acknowledges our ancestors and our roots.

"I went to an inauguration at UWC and there was a coloured school choir that sang some African songs. Archbishop Tutu, the chancellor at UWC, got up and said it was wonderful. 'When coloured children begin to learn our songs, we can truly say we are proud to be South Africans,' he said. It struck me then that it is always when coloured people adopt the African culture that they are qualified to be true South Africans. It never happens the other way around.

"I think coloured people have been pathologised pre-1994 and post-1994. It is an easy excuse to discriminate against coloured people. Coloured people were marginalised before 1994. They were co-opted by the apartheid government in several ways, for instance through housing subsidies, through the CRC [Coloured Persons Representative Council] and through the Labour Party. But blacks were also cooperative. The IFP [Inkatha Freedom Party] was co-opted before 1994; the whole Zulu population was co-opted.

"But that's not the point. The point is that, in the new South Africa, I never thought that I would become a defender of the right of coloured people to exist. I am shocked by myself pleading for people to understand where racism among coloured South Africans emanates. I think that coloured people are not treated fairly in terms of the new dispensation, in the slicing of the cake. It is not only about resources. It is about power. Coloured people have never been given power in terms of their own right."

Leo de Souza and Obed Zilwa

Leo de Souza described herself as outgoing and straightforward. "I am not scared of change. I am a very open person," she said. She saw this as both a strength and a weakness.

"My mom was Afrikaans and my dad Portuguese. Without them realising it, we had quite a cross-cultural upbringing. We were very mixed. We spoke English and Afrikaans. I went to an English school. My mother and father tried to put us in church, but it was the Catholic Church and not the normal church that Afrikaners went to. My dad was not very religious. So we grew up to be very open.

"My oldest brother is an executive at one of the major banks, extremely successful and very conservative. My baby brother is beautiful, artistic and gay, and I am who I am.

"I said to my mother that she or my dad must never ever ask what they did wrong. They must always ask what they did right. They produced three children, who are all extremely successful in their diverse ways. We are who we are and we have our own identities. They allowed us to explore, without realising it.

"This is not to say that Obed was not a shock to them. He was a big shock."

Leo's husband Obed Zilwa, who is of Xhosa descent, said he was a person willing to face challenge. "I have never been racist, never ever. I have been angry about the things which were different between the races, and angry about society. I guess this was one of the reasons why I left school. One of the reasons was that my mother was struggling. The other was that there was a need for somebody to tell the real stories of the township."

Obed started as a photographer at the *Cape Times* in the early 1980s. "There were very few *Cape Times* people in the township at the time. We needed to have somebody inside to tell our stories.

"I love to meet people and to understand people, whether this one is racist, or whether that one thinks differently about me because I am black. One of my neighbours, as soon as I moved in [to what was formerly a white area], told me that a piece of my land was his land and that I should back off. I discovered later that the land was in fact my land and that he had disobeyed municipal regulations."

Obed felt that the best way to deal with racism was to get to know the people who live next door to you. "A neighbour came to ask me to join the neighbourhood watch, which I did. I joined because I wanted to show that I am a South African and I want to do something about the area in which I am living.

"When I joined the *Cape Argus*, there was a photographer called Hannes Thiart, who was so Afrikaans. He used to tell me that if his mother knew he shared a desk with me, she would spit in his face. Today, he is still my best buddy."

Leo continued: "Obed and I are of a similar age. We discovered that while our upbringing was different, there were also many things we had in common. We both watched *Heidi* on television; we knew the same kind of songs, ate the same things and drank the same cooldrinks. Yes, there are differences, but these are cultural differences, not skin-colour differences."

Obed believed that Xhosas and Afrikaners were not that different to each other. "There are so many similarities in the way I was raised and the way Leo was raised. I think the only difference was in the language. They spoke Afrikaans, we spoke Xhosa. Maybe there were also affordability factors, because they were middle class and we were poor, but the messages we got from our mothers were similar. For instance, don't throw away food, because other people are hungry."

I told them about my own experience when I was editing the edition of the *Sunday Times* aimed at Soweto. I often used to sit with a columnist called Doc Bikitsha and discuss his column. I discovered then that the coloured people from Cape Town had a lot in common with the African people from Gauteng. For instance, we had the same superstitions. One of these superstitions was that if you came home late at night, you should enter backwards and throw salt over your shoulder.

Obed and Leo said that they implemented different parts of each other's culture in their lives. "For instance, Leo had to meet with the African women and become a Xhosa woman, which was a whole ritual thing," said Obed. "She even has a Xhosa name. She had to do this before she could put on that white dress and become my wife, before she could become an *umakoti* [a young wife]."

Leo said she accepted these customs and participated in them in a way in which she felt comfortable. "I am not going to force it and

Obed does not force me. Whenever we have certain functions, I need to dress up. I need to wear a scarf, because I need to look like an *umakoti*. It is a bit strange, but it is okay."

Asked about whether their description of themselves differed from the way other people described them, Obed said: "We hear different things from different people. You will find young kids who look at us and wish they could be like us. Then you will find people who think it is wrong for a black man to marry a white woman.

"The flower sellers in town will stop us in the middle of the street and say: 'Mandela has fixed all of this.' Then you go to Evander where the people look at you and just want to spit. You can tell by their faces. They hate it when they see a white woman with a black man. What I like about this is that it is better to know how they feel than to be in the dark."

Leo added: "Obed and I are similar in that we don't really care what people think of us. We are ourselves and it does not actually matter what others think. We are the type of people who feel that either you like us or you don't ..."

Leo believed some black women found it difficult to accept a black man marrying a white woman. "I think black women see a successful black man as a commodity that is lost to them.

"A lot of people aren't comfortable with us at first, but when they get to know us, that changes. Sometimes people are scared that we will judge them – especially white people. The most amazing thing is that since Nikki was born, when we are walking in the street, everyone wants to see what the baby looks like."

Asked if they ever had to deal with derogatory descriptions of themselves, both responded: "Yes, many times."

Leo explained: "We went to the west coast once, where Obed was going to take pictures of crayfish walking out of the sea. I decided to skip work and go with him. I booked into this small hotel in Elands Bay. When I made the booking, I spoke Afrikaans.

"When we got there, Obed was carrying the baby. This guy looked at Obed and said, 'Yes?' I said, 'We booked in' and he let us go past. After that we went to go sit in the bar. We got very bad service in the bar, but that was okay. Then we went to the dining room and there was this coloured guy who said, 'We don't get many people like you here.' We went to the bar again afterwards and I don't know what happened, but this one guy turned around and said to Obed: '*Kyk hierso*, Kaffer' [Look here, Kaffir]."

Obed interjected: "He was wearing this jacket with the old South African flag on it. He swore and pointed to the flag and said: '*Kyk, hier is* Mandela *se poeslappie* [Look, here is Mandela's sanitary pad].' He went on and on and we just sat there. Then another guy came up to me and asked me where I was from. I said I was from Cape Town and he asked me what I was doing in Elands Bay. I told him that I was with my family. He started calling me 'Kaffir'. Eventually they came up really close – there were about five of them, all Afrikaners, Boere. They were looking at me and I thought I was going to get *donnered* [clobbered] right there.

"I spoke to them in Afrikaans, which they hated as well. Eventually I cracked a joke with them. I then went to the barman and asked him whether he had Jack Daniels. I said he must give the five gentlemen each a double Jack Daniels. They first did not know where it was coming from. Eventually they asked the barman and he pointed to me. As they looked my way, I said 'cheers' and that broke the ice. Later they came to sit with us. They said they wanted to drink with me and make friends with me. But I still didn't trust them. I thought, everybody is smiling, so let's get out right now."

Leo continued: "The next morning at breakfast the owner came to us, smiling, and asked how our stay was. We told him it was not nice and he should sort out these things if he wanted more clientele.

"The next day we went to Lamberts Bay where they had a Protea Hotel. That night we went for supper. We sat down and waited for 15, 30 minutes. Eventually we called the waiter, who took our order and left. We continued to wait, while all the people around us were eating. They were all white. Eventually Obed called the waitress and asked what was going on. We asked whether we could have a drink, because we had been waiting for more than two hours. We did not get any joy from the waitress and Obed asked to see the manager. The manager told us if we did not like the hotel, we could leave.

"We went to our room, picked up our stuff and left. We'd had drinks earlier and had made a few telephone calls, but we refused to pay for them. We told them to lay a charge against us if they wished. We went to the police station which was next door and told them our story. The policeman on duty, a white guy, said that they always had these problems in their town. We drove all the way to Clanwilliam. The hotel there was also run by Afrikaners, but as soon as they heard our story, they gave us the most beautiful room. What I am trying to explain is that people are different: not all black people are the same, just as one white person is different to the next."

Leo said she felt welcome in the townships. Most of the racial problems she had experienced involved white and coloured people.

In answer to my question about honouring one's identity, Leo said that she felt it was important not to have a cultural identity that excluded other people. "I can never deny the fact that I am white, but that does not make me exclusive. So many times I forget that I am white. I call our family a black family. However, I am white, and my cultural heritage is very white. Obed's cultural heritage is very different. But I am allowed in and others are allowed in.

"I think about this a lot. For instance, it is very difficult to get into the Jewish culture if you are not born a Jew. Muslims are different and they allow you in. But all these groups run the danger of becoming exclusive and thus becoming racist."

Obed believed that the Zulu and Xhosa cultures were inclusive. "Any person, black or white, can come and enjoy our culture."

Wilmot James

"I would describe myself as a South African of mixed heritage, a Capetonian and a coloured."

Asked if his description of himself differed from the way other people described him, Wilmot said that, on a professional level, there was a difference as to how he saw himself. "I think there is a difference and especially recently I often find myself thinking that the perception other people have of me is not the same perception I have of myself.

I have the feeling that I am being treated like a coloured person in a stereotypical sense.

"Non-racialism was a myth, but it was a myth that served a good purpose in mobilising people across the colour spectrum. Once we settled down into a normal country and a normal state, you found that people just reverted back to their old sense of identity.

"One of the things that has happened in South Africa is that people who never used to classify themselves in terms of race, now suddenly find that they have to do this. One of the reasons for this is that the government needs to collect employment equity statistics, which will help them in addressing employment inequalities."

Wilmot felt that this could have contributed to the new sense of identity among South Africans. "During the apartheid years, when you gave your race, it had no consequences. In the new environment, there is a need to register whether people are eligible for certain benefits. And you don't want to cut yourself out of eligibility by not completing those racial forms.

"There is also a sense that there is a need to collect statistics to monitor progress of people on the equity stakes. But I think we are lazy in collecting these statistics and fall back on the conventional ways of describing ourselves."

Wilmot said that the most offensive description he'd had to deal with was being called a "Hotnot". "But that was a long time ago," he added.

He related an incident that took place in the late nineties, when he was walking with his fair-skinned daughter in Rondebosch. "Gaby must have been about seven at the time and this old white lady walked up to her and asked her whether this man was her father. To her credit, Gaby replied 'Of course he is' and the old woman just walked away. This old woman did not put it into words, but it was clear that she thought I was misleading a white child. That was humiliating. It was not a verbal description, but an assumption that because I was a coloured, I must be a criminal.

"Another interesting thing happened when I met the Director-General for Education, Thami Mseleku. He kept on greeting me as

'James'. After a while, I said to him that James was my last name and my first name was Wilmot. He apologised and said he did not mean to offend me. He said that in the Zulu culture, greeting someone by their clan name is indeed an honour. But I wanted to say to him that, in my culture, calling someone by his last name is highly insulting.

"I remember when I was very small, my father used to take his VW Beetle for servicing to a white Afrikaans mechanic living in Parow. This guy was a big racist and he always addressed my father as 'James'. I used to watch my father cringe and I could feel his humiliation. I remember that quite powerfully and I think that was why I reacted to Thami in that way. But Thami did not mean it at all and, in fact, he was quite serious. But there is no reason why his cultural presumptions should have any precedence over mine and we just need to communicate about that."

Wilmot also remembered his mother being called *meid* (pronounced "mate"), a derogatory term for black women. I asked him whether he thought there was still a lot of blatantly racist language around or whether people were learning to tone down their comments. Were people becoming more sensitive?

"I think there is a lot more sensitivity in the public domain, but who knows what happens in private. A lot of this negative terminology gets reinforced by the strange phenomenon of people referring to people who are similar to them in derogatory terms. For instance, black people in America, African-Americans, call each other 'nigger', and this is not seen as an insult."

Asked how one balances the conflicting demands of identity with racism, Wilmot responded, "There is a sense of cultural superiority in some people that is just offensive. This is something that you find a lot among English-speaking whites who take for granted a sense of superiority as a result of a civilised European heritage.

"I don't know what to do about it. Multiculturalism is fine, but when it comes to a sense of superiority because of ethnic chauvinism, then it becomes a problem."

Naledi Pandor
Naledi Pandor, speaking at the IJR's conference on race and identity,

described herself as a "cockney girl who likes *umngqusho* [samp]".

"I like to describe myself as a cosmopolitan African. I am also a Muslim. My religion is very important to me. We grew up in a very religious environment. It was a Christian environment, and I only became a Muslim when I got married.

"I like to believe that I am cosmopolitan and that I would feel at home in London, in Botswana, in Lesotho or even in the Muslim community on the Cape Flats."

Asked about derogatory descriptions she'd had to put up with, Naledi said: "Once, in London, a girl called me a nigger. That was the most offended I have ever felt and I hit that girl. It was the first and only time I ever resorted to violence."

Naledi believed her background had an effect on the way people related to her in society. "There are many African people who know that I am the granddaughter of [former ANC president] Z. K. Matthews and this causes them to behave in a certain way towards me."

Asked how one remains true to one's identity without being racist, Naledi said this was a difficult question to answer. "I think you have to put basic principles in place. For instance, if I accept that each one of us has rights, then I must accept the whole range of rights. I should be able to practise what I believe in and surely we should be able to live with each other. You cannot expect me to relate to you only by doing exactly what you do. That is difficult.

"For instance, some people in my community fight with me about abortion and the fact that the ANC is pro-choice on abortion, while Muslims do not support abortion. But the reality is that if something happens to one of their daughters, then it is good that they have this choice. They say that they are going to teach their daughter differently so that they would not have to make that choice, but anything can happen.

"I think it has to do with principles and being able to be different, to be able to practise our different religious and cultural practices. For instance, my son is amused that big boys go for circumcision, because he was circumcised when he was a baby. But we have to learn to accept that people have different identities."

"When we were still all in the academic sphere, Merlin Mehl [a former UWC professor] always used to begin his speeches by saying that he was a coloured who was not so-called. I could never understand what he meant, but he was saying that there is an identity and you need to deal with me in terms of my identity.

"Coloured people see themselves as coloured and they are indeed different in that way. That difference does not mean that they must treat others badly, but people need to accept who they are.

"Many people reject their community, their practices and the people they identify with. You need to accept your identity, and then you can work with people."

Melanie Verwoerd

Melanie Verwoerd described herself as a "realistic optimist".

"I need to dream, but not in an unrealistic sense. I absolutely passionately believe that things can change for the better. In that sense I am a real optimist. That is most probably how I would describe myself. And I am restless, and I don't seem to accept that things must stay the way they are."

And how did she describe herself from a racial and cultural perspective? "I describe myself as an African. I know it sounds fashionable, but I really feel that way. When I lived in Britain, I missed everything about Africa. When I am away, I do feel completely lost. I miss the sun, the sea, the people, the earth, the rain and everything about Africa.

"But then I would say that, obviously, I am a South African. Yes, I am from an Afrikaner background, but that is not my prime identity. I certainly don't feel comfortable with the traditional Afrikaner community. Even within an often enlightened Afrikaner community, I find myself feeling very alienated."

Melanie believed that while it was important for some people to have ways of defining themselves, this could become an easy tool for racism and stereotyping people. "People have multiple identities. They can choose to what extent they want a particular identity. Some people choose to be one hundred per cent within the Afrikaner cultural space and everything that goes with that, but they choose that consciously.

"There was a question in the newspapers about whether whites could call themselves Africans. The question should be about what you mean by African. Can you define yourself or do other people define you?

"The same thing is going on in Northern Ireland. People are struggling with identity. Are they Protestant or Catholic? Are they Irish or British? People get a sense of security from simplicity, but the one thing that we have learnt in South Africa is that simplicity is not always the answer. Maybe one should feel comfortable with the complexity. We South Africans are the primary examples of complexity in terms of our identities."

Asked if her description of herself differed from the way other people described her, Melanie said that there were people who thought that because she was a white ANC member, she must have been criticised by people within the ANC. "Again, this is very complex. I don't think I have been singled out as a white in the ANC – not for special treatment or to be given a hard time."

Melanie said she'd had to endure negative comments from the white community. "There were lots – it was fast and furious. It was mainly political things, like people calling me a traitor. I don't mind. I think I have shown that not all Afrikaners are the same."

Melanie said it was clear that her background played a role in determining how people related to her. "People have perceptions of what we are, where we come from and the language we speak. Particularly when your surname is Verwoerd. It is just such a visible surname. It always brings out a reaction in people. Most of the time, however, the reaction has been positive."

I asked her why she adopted the Verwoerd name, when she must have had a choice. She explained that this was not the case. "In 1987, it was not easy to do. It is very uncommon in the Afrikaner community for women not to adopt their husband's surnames. But it was also a personal issue. My parents were divorced and I had taken on my father's surname quite late. I did not feel really comfortable with that surname. When I married Wilhelm, it was the common thing to take his surname."

Melanie related my question about balancing identity with racism to the Klein Karoo Nasionale Kunstefees, an annual arts and cultural festival which is held in Oudtshoorn. The aim of the festival is to promote Afrikaans.

"This has been a difficult question. On the one hand, there is nothing inherently wrong with Afrikaans. I speak Afrikaans and my kids speak Afrikaans at home. At the same time, there is nothing wrong with cultural festivals, so there actually can't be anything inherently wrong with this festival. But again, it is how one practises something. If an Afrikaner festival becomes a way of mobilising on the one hand and excluding on the other, then I think it is completely wrong and it shouldn't happen. But if it is a celebration which does not claim to be exclusive and rather says, 'We are willing to change, we are willing to acknowledge, we will bring people together and our Afrikaner celebration does not exclude part of our complex identity,' then I don't have a problem with it.

"It is the same as something like Orania. I am sure that Carel will argue that what they are doing is not inherently racist, but it is. We all have the right to live our cultural identity, but it is about finding the right balance."

Trevor Oosterwyk

Trevor Oosterwyk would only describe himself in two ways: as a coloured and as a South African.

Asked if this differed from the way other people would describe him, he said: "I would like to describe myself as an African, but I don't. The majority of [South African] society describes themselves as African. They do this even more than they would describe themselves as South African. I feel sad that this identity, of being an African, is not given to me.

"It seems this African identity is not one that I can just claim. I would like to claim it, but my claiming it does not mean that I am going to get it, because the force outside me is greater than my ability to claim that identity. I thought I should have a right to it. Inasmuch as Xhosa people have a right to an African identity, Khoi people, who form a part of me, were the first people of Africa in southern Africa. Yet, this is a debate that is not held in South African society."

The most offensive descriptions Trevor had had to deal with were "*gam*" and "bushy", both terms used to ridicule coloured people. But he pointed out that black people also used derogatory terms in a non-derogatory way. "The other day I was writing a piece on the Arabisation of Islam in the Cape. I wrote about how certain words are disappearing and being replaced by Arab words. I wrote about 'Slams' [a derogatory term for Muslims] and how words like '*shukraan*' [thank you] and Eid have replaced Malay words such as '*tramakassie*' and '*Labarang*'. In our community it was okay to call people 'Slams' but if white people called you that, it was regarded as derogatory. A white news editor became upset with me and I had to explain to her that we call ourselves 'coloureds' and 'Slams' and it is fine. If she, however, decided to use those words, it would be seen as racist.

"When we use these words we are stripping them of their potential to be derogatory. It is not the words themselves that are problematic, but the way they have been used by people to advantage themselves or to advance racist ideas."

Asked if his background made a difference in terms of how people related to him, Trevor said: "I have had the good fortune of receiving an education and being involved in politics. People are a bit nervous to be derogatory to my face or to be racist, because I would be able to challenge them. I would say that my background, living and working in Cape Town, being a coloured, is far more acceptable than being African, particularly for white people, who relate to coloured people much more easily. I think this is because we speak the same language."

Trevor felt that the coloured identity has always been problematic. "We need to find some sense of a stable identity for this community. This is important for those in the middle classes so that they can feel the acceptance of who they are, their history and their experiences in life, and that society acknowledges that history and experience. They can then become settled in the knowledge of who they are. There must be a greater awareness of making everybody feel a part of our society. I am not too worried about coloured people in Cape Town.

I am more worried about the fact that Xhosa people do not feel part of our city.

"Coloured people always had a particular relationship with black people. That relationship was defined, for instance, by the milkman (who was always black) or the lady who came to iron, the maid. That was our understanding of black people. They were also people who spoke a strange language. I was always fascinated by the fact that from where I lived in Bonteheuwel, I could see the entrance to Langa. I knew that black people stayed there. I met them on the trains, but I never met a black person with whom I could establish a relationship. The closest I came was probably the 1978 period when I began to go to Gugulethu to visit a family that I had met in the church and not through politics.

"We also had a certain relationship with white people. We revered them, because they were the bosses, the 'larneys'. There were the white people, then there was us, and the black people stood at the other end of the scale. That is how we understood our place in society as a people.

"The social and political distance between us and them [Africans] was miles apart. I make this point because on the one hand there was this claim that we were all black. On the basis of that claim, there was an expectation that we should understand each other as coloured and African, and that there should be some sort of unity between us. But that notion had no basis in reality. It has had no basis for many years for a lot of people. We are really talking about two different groups of people here. If one wants to think about it in tribal terms, then it is like the Xhosas and the Tswanas. They are really two different sets of people, even though they would call themselves black and African. You begin to delve into the social relations between those groups and you find that there are more differences than similarities. Between coloureds and Africans these differences are even greater.

"I make that point also because at a later stage we were made to feel guilty about being coloured. It was seen as a bad identity and an identity that was reactionary. At the time I did not understand that, but in the 1980s, particularly in the struggle, it was said that claiming to be coloured was a reaction and we should not call ourselves coloureds.

We did not understand it at the time, but this denial of our identity alienated us from the very people who, for instance, gave birth to us and who were our friends.

"We became friends with black people and white people and got swept up into this notion of a black national democratic revolution. We failed to show our community that there was no contradiction between being coloured and being involved in the struggle. We had to deny our colouredness and pursue what we thought was a non-racial position. We were never able to be called coloureds and we became critical of our parents, our sisters and brothers, and we were sometimes embarrassed by them. We did not like to take our friends home, particularly our African friends, because we thought they would think our families were racist.

"For us, politics was not only about theory; it was not about reading books or about having the correct understanding. It was more about being in the trenches and fighting the fight that we had to fight. We believed that it was only in action that we would be able to work these things out, but we never did.

"A lot of people became involved in the struggle. There was a shift in the community to a greater acceptance of the UDF kind of organisation. There was an identity emerging in that mass movement that was going to be different. It was not going to be a sectarian coloured or a sectarian African or Xhosa identity. People were a whole lot more accepting of each other. Unfortunately, this identity was not allowed to grow and develop in a more tangible, substantial way. But I saw this in the mid-1980s and I was quite excited by this.

"That is in part why I was in a sense paralysed by the results of the 1994 elections [when the ANC lost the Western Cape to the National Party]. This is why I say that we over-estimated the support that we [the ANC] had. There is no denying that if there had been an election in 1984, 1985 or 1986, we would probably have won hands down, because I believe we had the support of the community at that time.

"But an identity in the making is always an unstable identity. The gains that you make can easily be rolled back. They can easily be undone. To some extent the political identity was rolled back in the post-1990 era. The silent majority who came out and voted had remained conservative throughout the 1980s."

Kenny and Sielie Nolan
Manenberg couple Kenny and Sielie Nolan said they would definitely describe themselves as coloured.

Both Kenny and Sielie felt that your background played a role in the way people related to you. "White people only see coloured people as workers. They don't see you as having another identity," said Sielie. She gave an example of a German man who had asked her to work for him. "I was supposed to work until 2 p.m., but when I got there I ended up working until 4 p.m. He did not consider that I also had a family to go home to. For him, I was just a worker."

Asked how she viewed her position in post-apartheid South Africa, Sielie replied, "It is clear to me that Africans now get the cream of society. For instance, African people get all the work, while coloured people struggle to find work."

Kenny understood this as part of correcting the injustices of society: "When I grew up, I saw how the African people struggled. The white man was on top and they were right at the bottom. Today they are getting all the opportunities."

Sielie added: "It is clear that African people have used the opportunities to educate themselves. In the old days, you never found African people in banks or in hospitals. Now you find them everywhere. In the old days, they just had to do the dirty work.

"The end of apartheid has been good for African people. It has uplifted them. I remember that African people only used to get pension every two months and that has changed. However, we coloured people find ourselves in the middle once again. With the Africans on top and whites at the bottom, we find that we still struggle to find work. So the end of apartheid has not benefited us in the same way."

I asked Kenny and Sielie whether they had explored their roots. It is common for coloured people to talk about their European roots, without declaring anything about their African heritage.

Sielie responded: "I have not looked into my own roots, but I know that many years ago, there had to have been a relationship between a black man and a white woman or a white man and a black woman. This is how we, as coloured people, came to exist."

Kenny added: "The amazing thing is that we are all different colours. Some of us are almost white and others very black. Maybe that is why they call us coloureds."

Vincent Barnes

Cricket coach Vincent Barnes described himself as an African as well as a South African citizen. "I would never classify myself as anything other than a human being. People speak quite lightly about how we have gone through different names for coloured people, from 'so-called coloured' to 'non-white'. We have gone through all these names, but I am just an ordinary person born in Africa and that is why I call myself an African."

Vincent believed his description of himself was close to how other people would describe him. "A friend of mine sent me an SMS after he saw that I got nominated for a national position in cricket. It simply said that I was possibly the only genuinely oppressed sportsman to have reached the greatest heights in sport. This was touching and made me aware that there are people who support me. Because you are a person of colour, you will always find that people doubt your abilities."

Asked if he'd ever had to deal with any offensive descriptions of himself, Vincent said he had had a turbulent time when he was at Livingstone High School in Cape Town in the 1980s. "Livingstone was a very strong school, politically, and we would have meetings and marches and the police would come and be abusive towards us, and call us insulting names. But this was to be expected.

He agreed that his background had an effect on the way people related to him. "In the field I am in, people always suspect that I am in my position because of my colour. White people who played cricket two, three years ago, are being nominated for senior positions in cricket, and nobody questions it. I have been coaching for more than 17 years, in South Africa and Scotland, but it never appears to be enough. White people are not comfortable with the fact that someone of colour can know so much about sport or lead a sport. There is no doubt that if I had been white, it would have been different."

Vincent said there were many people who questioned his position, saying that he had never played cricket at the highest level. Yet this was not possible because of apartheid. "When I was at my peak, I was not allowed to play at the highest level. I was not prepared to forsake my principles and join an apartheid club."

Athena and Manny Sotomi

Athena Sotomi described herself as "a South African and a black woman: a black female South African with a coloured experience, if you want to talk about race. I can't deny what is part and parcel of who I am."

Her husband Manny chipped in and said that there had always been a debate around the existence of a coloured race. Athena responded, "This debate is going to rage for a long time because the coloured community, if you want to call it that, is going through a huge amount of change in this country at the moment."

Manny said he was shocked to arrive in South Africa for the first time to discover "a very unusual group of people called 'coloured'". He explained, "I had met Athena in Britain. In Britain and America she was black, but when I arrived here I discovered that she was coloured."

"I tried to tell you," said Athena, "but you were too in love."

Manny continued: "It came as a shock to me, because in Angola and Nigeria, people with a lighter skin like hers were still considered black."

Athena added: "Everything in Britain was a liberating experience. It was good to be called black regardless of how light-skinned you were. Yet not everyone was so lucky. I had a friend who had a very light skin and she was always complaining about being ostracised by the black community in Britain."

Asked how he would describe himself, Manny said: "I am an African first and foremost. I have deep roots in Africa. I did not grow up in Africa, but this continent is where I feel at home."

Asked if her description of herself differed from the way other people described her, Athena replied: "It depends on who the people are. Overseas I am just another black woman, but here people relate to you differently."

She recounted what happened to her at the Home Affairs office in Cape Town one day. "I was standing in the queue and there was a coloured woman behind the counter. She was so rude about an African man and she said 'we', meaning her and me. I said, 'Excuse me, what is this "we" business? Don't think that because I look like you, I think like you.'"

Athena said that a white woman had once called her a "packhorse". "It was a long time ago, I was in my twenties, but I shall never forget."

Manny commented: "Because of my character, people do not call me names. For instance, if someone decides to call me 'Kaffir', I will probably put him down. I am not shy. I have done it before. I will knock his block off. This is probably why I do not hear first-hand descriptions of me. I normally just deal with it."

Manny thought that the couple's background had impacted on the way people related to them in society. "When we first arrived in South Africa, we were stared at a lot. People were very interested to see what our baby looked like. And when I spoke, people would stop and want to speak to me. They would say: 'Are you from America or are you from Britain?' I normally became very hostile in these instances, because the reaction to hearing my accent, following the initial reaction to my appearance, was very superficial.

"A while ago my brother, who lives in San Francisco, came to visit. He had this Caucasian girlfriend and they got a lot of stares, even in this day and age, after liberation. Someone even tried to run them over in our neighbourhood. I just said to them: 'Welcome to South Africa.'"

With regard to honouring one's own and one another's identities, Athena said that exploring each other's cultures would help to create tolerance. "South Africans have just woken up from a long sleep and need to discover this big world out there. We need to explore each other's cultures more."

Manny added: "There is a danger in creating a group of South Africans who don't speak the indigenous languages of South Africa. This is when that balancing act becomes necessary. My eldest son, for instance, describes himself as Nigerian, even though he has never been there. I have not lived in Nigeria for a long time, but that is still my cultural identity.

"How do I balance that with racism? In my culture, there is what the South Africans call *ubuntu*, which dictates that I respect people for who they are. So I have never had a problem balancing my own identity with racism."

Khusta and Karen Jack

Khusta and Karen Jack described themselves as South Africans: "Strong South Africans". However, Khusta said he also saw himself as a "black South African". Karen was a bit more hesitant. "We don't really like to use the white–black label so much with the kids, because they are not black and they are not white."

Asked if their description of themselves differed from the way other people described them, Khusta said: "We are lucky in a number of ways. People seem to accept us as perhaps the South Africa that we ought to be, because we came into being at the doorstep of the new South Africa.

"I have never heard anybody call us anything. They regard us as South Africans. I don't think the kids think they are anything else. They will not accept it if you say they are coloured, black or white. They just want to be South African."

Karen interjected: "Although Themba does say that Kayla is white." Khusta replied: "Yes, but that is because of her skin colour."

Karen continued: "When people say a black guy did this and that, it's jarring to me, because I feel uncomfortable with this whole colour labelling thing."

Khusta felt that we inherited racial labels. "There are a lot of bad things happening around racism," he said. "Non-racialism has just gone out the window. There is a race for resources. I wonder what would have happened if South Africa's economy was overheating, bubbling and strong? Things would have been different. What happens now is that if an African person does not get something, he says: 'I did not get it because I am black.' If a coloured person does not get it, he will say: 'It is because I am not black enough' and the white guy will say: 'It is obvious that I am not black.'

"All the differences between people in South Africa are now being exploited, and that is because of limited resources. If we had a lot of resources, nobody would have been worried about what is happening. Once people are depressed, they will think of everything that can divide them. That is a problem in South Africa."

Khusta said they had never had to deal with derogatory remarks. "It helps when high-profile people such as me or people like Tokyo Sexwale have non-racial marriages. If you have high-profile black people who are rooted strongly and who have credentials that are unquestionable within the black community, it makes life easier.

"It helps when we are economically strong. If, for instance, you had a mixed marriage and you had to contend with poverty, people would victimise you and your children. I am strong financially, politically, academically and in every other facet. Because of this, we don't have to deal with these kinds of insults."

Asked if their background had impacted the way people related to them in society, Khusta said: "I have a very high profile, especially in Port Elizabeth and the Eastern Cape. Wherever I go, people know who I am. This reduces the chance of people adopting a negative attitude towards me."

Asked how one remains true to one's identity, Khusta said: "People have the right to their own cultural identity. We must just find a way of balancing this."

Karen added: "We have to bring our different cultural identities to the mainstream, so that everyone can enjoy bits of each other's culture and be proud to be South African. Different cultures should not be locked away and kept on their own. This can be done through the media. The different facets of different cultures can be brought together and celebrated as a sort of popular culture, whether in song or in language. There must be a concerted effort to make this part of everybody's experience."

Tracy-Lee Rosslind

Tracy-Lee Rosslind described herself as "passionate about my morals and beliefs. I am a very caring person and I am very open-minded.

"I can't say that I am completely non-racist, because I would be lying. I do notice differences between people and I do make comments on those differences. Sometimes I find that African people speak loudly and that irritates me, because I was raised to believe that you do not raise your voice in public. But I actually go to them and I say, 'I understand that you are not supposed to be whispering, but we must come to a compromise.' I can't say I am race free. I do acknowledge there are differences, but I accept those differences."

I asked her how she would describe herself from a racial perspective. "I look at myself as a coloured South African," Tracy-Lee said, "but one day I would like to say I am South African and forget about the black and the white and the coloured. However, at the moment I see myself as coloured."

I asked her whether her description of herself corresponded with the way other people saw her. "If you are talking about personal descriptions of me, then the answer is 'yes'. But if you are talking about people's descriptions of me as a coloured person, then the answer is 'no'. Everybody sees coloureds in rollers with a *doekie* [scarf] over their heads, with no teeth in their mouths, walking down the road with four children wrapped around their hips and their ankles. I get very upset because the white kids at school like to make fun of the coloured accent. They try to talk to each other like coloureds. But coloureds don't even talk the way they think we talk, and they see it as a joke."

I asked her if she thought her background influenced people's reactions to her. She said that because of her strong ANC background (both her parents were activists within the ruling ANC), people called her a politician at school. "I am always trying to educate the other kids as best I can. If I was white, I think my words would sink in easier. They would say that I understand what I am talking about. But because I am black, it is more difficult to convince them. To most of the white kids, apartheid is a textbook issue, but to us it is different. It is something we lived and experienced."

Regarding identity, Tracy-Lee said: "We are different. I am coloured. You must be proud of the fact that you are black, of the fact that you are coloured. However, you must love the other races for who they are and for their strengths, because we all have strengths and weaknesses, and not because of the colour of our skins.

"It all boils down to our cultures and traditions. But when you try to put a person down because of their race, then it is racism. If you are describing somebody, you are not being judgemental and you are not putting them down. That wouldn't be considered as being racist because you are just expressing that person's outward appearance so that somebody else could get a visual of that person."

I asked Tracy-Lee whether there was such a thing as a coloured consciousness. "Yes, there is," she said. "Our culture is in the way we look at our religion, the way we interact with each other. White people and black people don't call their family together on a Sunday to have roast. Even though it is something so small, that is something that most coloureds do. We love our family and we love all being together. If I look at the way white kids interact with their parents, it is clear to me that the whole family unit is made up so differently to a coloured family. We seem to be closer to one another than the white families. We also love food. We did a survey on this [at school] and found that coloured people spend more money on food than white people do. So I think there are cultural differences."

Keathelia Satto

Keathelia Satto was the only interviewee who described herself as a "coloured and a Christian". She said she had heard other people describing her as black. "At primary school I used to get upset about it, but now that I am at high school, I feel I can insult them back."

She did not believe that her background influenced the way people treated her in society.

My thoughts

It is clear from these interviews that many South Africans are grappling with their identities. None of the people I interviewed could give me definitive descriptions of themselves. In some ways, South Africans always seem to make excuses before describing themselves. For instance, I always describe myself as a human being, a South African and maybe as a black South African. However, I know that most of the people with whom I interact would probably describe me as a coloured, and not even as a "so-called coloured". Yet the fact that I feel uncomfortable about being called a coloured does not mean that this group does not exist. There are definitely many people in South Africa who feel comfortable, even proud, of being called coloured.

The important point here is that people must feel free to call themselves what they want. So, for instance, if a white South African wants to call herself an African, she must be entitled to do so, because, after all, if she was born in Africa, then she is an African. The difficulty is when other people impose an identity on you, as mentioned in several of the interviews, most notably those with Phatekile Holomisa and Melanie Verwoerd.

I chose the questions I asked in this chapter because these are questions that have always fascinated me. For instance, when I asked "How do you describe yourself?" I did not initially ask "How do you describe yourself in racial and cultural terms?" Yet most of the respondents assumed I was asking them to describe themselves in racial terms and did so without hesitation though also, in some cases, with discomfort.

The issue of derogatory descriptions is one with which most black South Africans can identify. All black South Africans have had to deal with derogatory descriptions of themselves at some point in their lives. In the coloured community in the Western Cape, derogatory descriptions are plentiful and, in some cases, they are used as a defence mechanism against racism from other groups. In much the same way as African-Americans use the word "nigger" to describe themselves, coloureds are increasingly using terms such as "*gam*". The idea is that taking ownership of these words makes it difficult for others to use them against you in a hurtful way.

Things are changing slowly, however, and as more African people move up in society, soon the only important colour will be the colour of their money. In many ways, this is already the case in Johannesburg, where black people, and in particular African people, have joined the mainstream economy.

The most difficult question that I asked, I think, was the one dealing with the issue of identity and race. It is important to accept that there are different cultures in South Africa. How much importance should be given to different races, however, is a tricky question. While one wants to encourage the development of different cultures, one cannot do so if this leads to or encourages racism. This is one of the reasons I decided to interview Carel Boshoff. I felt I needed to understand the logic of having a whites-only homeland in post-apartheid South Africa. Most of what Carel said made sense, and I don't believe that he can be convinced otherwise. "All I am trying to do," he said, "is to protect my culture."

But as I was listening to Carel, I remembered a conversation I'd had with some of the most notorious gang leaders in the Western Cape, while I was editor of the *Cape Times*. They came to see me to complain that we were misrepresenting them. They told me how they wanted to work with government and how they were providing jobs for people in the community who would not be able to find work otherwise. One of these gang leaders spoke about a man with a Grade Four education, who had just come out of prison and who had a wife and four children. "Who will employ this man if I don't?" asked the gang leader. As I listened to him and his colleagues, I had to remind myself all the time that I was not speaking to reasonable men, but to gang leaders, murderers, rapists and drug dealers. No matter how well they articulated their arguments, you could not divorce them from their backgrounds. This was very much the way I felt as I listened to Carel. No matter how well he articulated himself, I still felt that racism was the major motivation behind Orania. But at least, after speaking to him, I had a much better understanding of his form of racism.

And this, I suppose, is one of the keys to understanding racism in post-apartheid South Africa: these days, racism is far more complex than it used to be. The great irony is that, over ten years since the formal abolition of apartheid, race is still as big an issue as ever (if not a bigger issue), and it still impacts on everything we do.

My feeling is that while the 1970s were about black consciousness, the 1980s were about non-racialism, and the 1990s were about reconciliation, the new millennium should be about rediscovering our identities, free from apartheid stigma. I think it is important to celebrate our diverse backgrounds and investigate our own heritage, but in an inclusive way. With these goals in mind, I believe that this could be the most exciting phase yet in our country's history.

CHAPTER 3
WHAT IS RACISM?

Are South Africans still racist?

Would you let your daughter marry a ...?
In the old South Africa, people would test one another's commitment to non-racialism with statements such as: "It's okay to have black friends, but would you let your daughter marry a black?" or "How would you feel if your son married an *iLawu* [a derogatory term for a coloured person]?"

I have often thought about this: is the fact that you are prepared to let a daughter marry someone from another racial group or the fact that you are prepared to sleep with a member of another race a sign of true non-racialism?

What is racism? Is it a system of a dominant group oppressing a weaker group (as whites did in South Africa for many years under apartheid) or is it possible to be racist even when you do not have the power to enforce your racism?

George M. Frederickson, in his book *Racism: A Short History*, states:

> The term 'racism' is often used in a loose and unreflective way
> to describe the hostile or negative feelings of one ethnic group
> or 'people' toward another and the actions resulting from such
> attitudes. But sometimes the antipathy of one group toward another

is expressed and acted upon with a single-mindedness and brutality that go far beyond the group-centred prejudice and snobbery that seems to constitute an almost universal human failing.

Under apartheid, we often argued that it was impossible for black people to be racist, because they were powerless to act on their racism, unlike the whites who had political and economic power. Recently, however, I have come to believe that it is in fact possible for black people to be racist, and that you can be racist even if you do not have the power to act on your beliefs.

This is why Nelson Mandela's statement at the Rivonia Trial was so profound. His assertion that he would oppose black domination in the same way that he had opposed white domination was possibly one of the most visionary statements made by a South African leader. Martin Luther King Junior echoed this statement when he said: "A doctrine of black supremacy is as evil as a doctrine of white supremacy."

Obviously there are different definitions of racism. For instance, Carel Boshoff and his followers do not believe they are racist to demand a white homeland in a liberated and politically black-controlled South Africa. They argue that they simply want to be with people who are similar to them. Is this racism, when people knowingly interact only with people who are similar to them? I have been to many parties in South Africa where there were only whites, only coloureds or only Africans. I've also been amazed at how easily the people at these almost racially-exclusive parties slip into talk of "them" and "us", without realising it.

My wife and I were the only black people at a dinner party in one of Cape Town's formerly white suburbs. The entire evening we listened to the white people at this party talk about what I can only describe as "white fears" – issues around crime and affirmative action. The startling thing for me was that most, if not all, of the people at this party considered themselves to be progressive. Most had been involved in the struggle against apartheid and some had even been in exile. One of the couples, who had been in exile, spoke about how they were thinking of emigrating because they could not face the many problems that we had in South Africa.

After attending that party, and several others like it, I thought about Carel Boshoff and his desire for a homeland, and I realised that maybe what he was asking for was not unreasonable. Maybe he and his people merely wanted to formalise what everybody else was practising. And perhaps if he had started his homeland without publicising it, nobody would have taken any notice, because most other people were practising racial exclusivity in their daily lives already.

But is racism still an issue, and are South Africans still racist? These are the questions that I put to the people I interviewed. I also asked them how they defined racism. The following are excerpts from some of their responses.

Trevor Oosterwyk

"Racism is a still a huge issue," said Trevor. "It is impossible to think that after 300 years of white domination, of European racism being forced on our society, of classism, we would be able to eradicate racism in the first decade of democracy. This is not possible. And even though legally there should be no racism, you still find in your everyday interactions with people that they are racist.

"My understanding is that the primary form of racism is the one related to power relations – having the power to be racist. You can call somebody this or that, and this would not amount to racism if you didn't have the power to take action. I don't agree that you can be racist if you do not have the ability to act against people on the basis of their race, or when you cannot negatively impact on their life. If I called you a Kaffir, but I did not have the ability to act on my notion of your being a Kaffir – for instance, if I could not deny you a job or arrest you on the basis of that notion – then that is not racism."

Trevor felt that racism remained an issue because there was still a hugely unequal ownership of and access to resources in South Africa.

"This is particularly so in the Cape, where the economy and the politics are still very much white dominated and controlled. Because of that white control, access to resources is still influenced by racial notions. In the struggle for those resources, the white community is complaining about black people moving up in society, and suddenly they are throwing a laager in defence of what they have and what they think people want to take away.

"In that sense, they still act in ways that are racist. You can see it in the workplace in the way white people deal with black people. Their public persona might be non-racial, because there is a law that governs these things, but when you scratch the surface and hear them talk among themselves, you will be surprised."

Melanie Verwoerd

"In a strange way, racism is less of a problem in our country than in some other places in the world," claimed Melanie. "This is because we are dealing with it consciously and because it is on the agenda all the time, because of our history. But of course, racism remains a problem. It is inside us and will probably remain inside all of us.

"I also believe that the language of racists has become more sophisticated. People will at least try to be decent in public, most of the time. I think many people have moved more to the middle, if you want to generalise. Obviously, there is a difference between us and the generation just above us who grew up under apartheid and who had a serious involvement in it, either by just being passive about it, by voting for the National Party, or by taking part in it. In this sense, they have to take some responsibility.

"But there seems to be a collective amnesia, perhaps because it is too painful to acknowledge what happened. People who are leaving the country say they are not racist, but they are leaving because of the new racism in South Africa. They say they want jobs and their children will not have opportunities in South Africa. This indicates for me a complete amnesia about the responsibility that we hold. And amongst the younger generation there is just no conception of the past.

"I don't think racism is going to disappear in my generation. There is nothing that irritates me more than people saying we must forgive and forget, and get on with the future."

Phatekile Holomisa

In Phatekile's opinion, tribalism had become more of an issue than racism. "For instance in the Eastern Cape, the Premier initiated a move towards the renaming of that part of our country. If we are looking at language, one would have expected the area to be called Xhosaland, because all the people living there, especially the blacks, can speak the Xhosa language.

"But Xhosas are not one. I am not Xhosa. I am Thembu. The Xhosas proper are the Baleka, the Gagabe and the people who lived on either side of the Kei River. The others originally spoke a dialect that was associated with Xhosa. These included the AmaThembu, AmaMpondo, AmaBatha, AmaHlubi, and a number of others.

"The missionaries introduced education and adopted Xhosa as an African language of instruction, because their first entry into the area was with the Xhosa. When they moved up to the other parts of the area they used Xhosa to educate the people there. Because of that, we all became Xhosa-speaking, but we are AmaBatha, and so on. The AmaMpondo, for instance, do not like to be referred to as Xhosa, because they see themselves as different.

"What I am saying is that before we can consider other races, there are issues within the African community that need to be dealt with.

"We have been fortunate, within Contralesa, to enjoy the support of the majority of traditional leaders in all the other tribes. But there have been instances where opposition to my position arose, not on the basis of what I have done or on the basis of my abilities, but mainly because I am Xhosa speaking. The others, who are ambitious to hold the position that I am holding, would say that they have been led by a Xhosa for too long. They would say: 'We are AmaShangaan, AmaMpondo or Basotho, and we are also capable of coming up with leaders who can lead us.' So you find that some positions are given to people merely in order to ensure the tribal balance and to avoid rumblings about there being too many Xhosas, or too many Zulus, or too many Sothos.

"When it comes to tribal fights, I understand that these fights are started by people who look down on others, who think they are superior. Wherever they go they will get themselves the best of whatever is available. They will hold onto enormous amounts of land, while the majority of their people live in overcrowded villages."

Phatekile said Africans also held stereotypical views of coloureds and Indians. "African people think you can't trust a coloured, because they always want to curry favour with the whites. They say the Indians are *skelms* [crooks] who can cheat you out of anything.

"Even among the tribes you will hear people saying things like the Xhosas are cunning, the Zulus like fighting and the Sothos are too submissive. I believe that the important thing is that we continue to interact with each other, because I am comfortable with all the other communities. When we are in Contralesa meetings, we joke about being Venda, Shangaan, Zulu or Tswana. But some people want to downplay their tribal identity and I don't think it [tribal identity] should be a problem.

"We have to acknowledge that we have cultural characteristics, that these are God-given, and that we are not responsible for them, because nobody chooses to be a member of any race or ethnic group."

"Racism also has to do with culture. I was attending a South African agricultural meeting and the hall was packed with white males. There were a few black individuals, mainly from the companies that support South African agriculture, and there were a few representatives from neighbouring countries. The president of the National African Farmers' Union spoke and, in the course of his speech, he related that he had a farm, but did not own any goats. The people who worked for him owned goats and those goats would graze on his farm. He had cattle, but the people who worked for him also owned cattle, which grazed on his farm. The president was advising the meeting that we should learn to share, because we have this problem of labour tenants, where some people do not necessarily work for the farmer, but because they are relatives, they live on the farm.

"In our culture we share. I could see from the body language of those white farmers at the meeting that they were not particularly interested in his speech, because they did not understand this concept of sharing.

"This question, which might generally be referred to as racism, has a lot to do with culture. The Europeans, to my understanding, are not used to sharing with others. They are acquiring and individualistic.

The capitalist system negates everything Africans believe in, which is to share. You are not expected to be rich while others remain poor. Not that it is wrong to be rich, but you should not be rich at the expense of the others. This does not apply with the Europeans. That is a problem.

"I think the problem lies in the differing attitudes of South Africans towards the sharing of wealth and resources. We cannot have a country having pockets of wealth in a sea of poverty."

Carel Boshoff

"Of course, one has to consider the history of South Africa," noted Carel. "My own perspective of racism would be different to the perspective of a coloured or African person, because my history and personal experiences were different. I was always on the privileged side of things, even though in the past I might not have been aware of it. I also know that there is a tendency among whites to mobilise people on the basis of reverse racism.

"Even though I can see that things like affirmative action, the shift in power, the redistribution of welfare and such things can have an impact on the white community, I am not personally inclined to use the rhetoric of reverse racism. I am of the opinion that the rhetoric should shift from the national categories that we had under apartheid and be continued on a local or community level, where people's welfare can be accommodated within the ambit of self-sufficient communities. I believe that such communities should be established, promoted and supported.

"There is a difference between the legacy of racism, and racism today. It is clear that the legacy of racism is still one of our biggest problems and that it lies behind the whole logic of transformation.

"Racism has the potential to become one of our biggest problems, but this is not my experience at the moment. There is a point where problems could seem like racism, but could be related to the cultural diversity and multilingualism of South Africa.

"In South Africa we have to accept that racism is something that emerges when the level of polarisation goes beyond a certain critical level. I don't think we are that polarised at the moment, but the possibility exists that we could become that polarised again.

"The Africanist rhetoric that sometimes comes from South Africa's leadership has the potential to be interpreted in racist terms. For instance, President Mbeki's attitude towards Zimbabwe could be as an expression of solidarity that defines itself in terms of Africa versus the West, but it could also be interpreted as white versus black or black versus white.

"This also relates to the concept of the Two Nations Theory of South Africa. There is a potential to develop a huge area of common ground between Africanism and Afrikaners' solidarity with Africa.

"But then we need action. Something needs to happen to make it happen. We cannot allow ourselves to be caught up in a polarising rhetoric, otherwise we will not be able to develop this common ground. We will continue to polarise up until the point where racism will once again become the most prominent characteristic of our society."

Rhoda Kadalie

Human rights activist Rhoda Kadalie described racism as "a system that privileges people on the basis of race".

"It is a system that privileges one race group above another," she said. "In South Africa we had a system of racial domination and racial superiority, and a legalised and structured system of discrimination.

"Unfortunately, there are such systems in most parts of the world. Racism has become a social and cultural norm and even when you abolish the legalised structural system of racism, the system remains intact because people are privileged. For example in South Africa, even though many of us were discriminated against as coloureds, Africans and Indians, many people had themselves reclassified in order to get a job. They used the very system that privileged others to privilege themselves. So every year people were racially classified voluntarily.

"It is purely a system; it's a construction of who people are and the way they are categorised, and it privileges some above others. With it go feelings of superiority on the basis of that privilege."

"You see it with immigrants coming in. There is a scramble for jobs and resources such as houses and land. So when you get foreigners, especially black foreigners, coming into our country, the very black people who were discriminated against in South Africa in the past are now discriminating against these people from other countries.

"You will also find that white South Africans will discriminate against foreign whites like Eastern Europeans, Italians and Portuguese. I think we do have discrimination and systems of superiority throughout our society.

"I think racism is a big problem. However, I do think that in 1994 there was a major realisation among white South Africans that they were wrong and apartheid was declared a crime against humanity internationally. I think white people were quite embarrassed about the fact that they supported a system that allowed the minority to oppress the majority. That is why today you won't find one white person who will admit to having supported that system.

"Also, I think our Constitution equalises us. The nice thing about the Constitution is that the person living in an informal settlement is equal to Nelson Mandela and equal to Thabo Mbeki.

"Finally, I think that things such as affirmative action, employment equity and human rights around race, diversity and social orientation are all attempts to redress the past. So even though racism is still a problem, there are mechanisms that are redressing the racial discrimination of the past. I also think that people are beginning to know how to use those mechanisms. When I was with the Human Rights Commission, we had a lot of complaints about racism. The Commission did not always deal with them properly, but many people did receive redress by using these mechanisms."

Athena and Manny Sotomi
Athena Sotomi said that racism was still "very much" alive in South Africa.

"There are ten thousand reasons I can give you. You walk into a shop and you don't always get served first, even if you were in the shop first, because the person next to you is white and they will get served first. The amazing thing is that the person behind the counter is often not a white person. But whether it is a white or black person, this kind of thing happens all the time.

Manny Sotomi intervened: "They ignore you. When they give you change, they put the money on the counter. I often say to them, 'I put the money in your hand, why can't you put it in my hand?' Athena is right, racism still exists, but I think the paradigm shift is starting; the norms are moving for everybody, and they are moving incredibly quickly.

"The problem that exists is a lot smaller than it was. A place like America was supposedly liberated in the fifties and sixties in terms of equal rights. South Africa is fast approaching that space and we'll overtake them if we continue at this pace. This is my personal perspective, having lived in both countries. The white people who live here will have to realise that this is Africa and that they have to accept that if they want to get ahead. The pockets of power and money still exist, and they will get ahead in those circles, anyway, with their own money. However, the young Afrikaner and the young black person know that they must work together to get ahead.

"The only problem I see is the fact that cultures are eroding and melting into one. You have young African kids who don't speak their indigenous languages. You have teenagers that come from wealthy African families who don't speak an African language. And you have young white people, Afrikaners, who sometimes can't speak Afrikaans. This is not necessarily a bad thing, but it would be a shame if we lost our cultures."

Wilmot James

Wilmot James described racism as "a presumption of inferiority or superiority or consequential difference based merely on appearance, principally skin colour". He agreed that racism was still a problem in South Africa "even though there have been major positive shifts in attitude in recent years".

"However," he said, "there are still extraordinary forms of exclusions that have nothing to do with constitutional laws or official policy. These happen on quite a wide scale and I think it's a problem."

He said that there was a difference in the levels of racism between the urban and rural areas of South Africa. "This has to do partly with the population and partly with culture. But education levels also play a role. The rural areas have less access to modern means of communication and more access to primitive ideas. But there are also some examples of people doing something about it, for instance farmers and their farm workers. I don't think that one can make any general statements about it."

Naledi Pandor

Naledi Pandor felt that racism would persist while political and economic power resided in different hands.

"It is not something that will disappear overnight. However, it depends on your definition of racism. If racism means the ability of a minority to use its power over a voiceless majority, then racism is no longer a major problem.

"These days there is also more subtlety when it comes to racism. It is no longer so overt. For instance, when I lived in Bophuthatswana, I once went into a white shop and was chased outside by the white shopkeeper. I did not know what was going on then. What was curious, however, was the way the local blacks watched me as I entered the shop, almost wanting to warn me that I should not go in there. Of course, all of this was foreign to me."

Kenny and Sielie Nolan

Sielie Nolan described travelling on a minibus taxi from Wynberg to her work in Constantia, the only coloured in a bus full of Africans. "All the talk is about race. It is about the way the white people treat them. It is about them being envious of the white people's money. I don't have a problem with white people having money, as long as they have worked for it. But the people on the taxi obviously have problems. They say things like: 'The madam wants to give me a peanut butter sandwich, but she can give that to her dog.' When the taxi stops, sometimes on a traffic circle or sometimes at a stop street, they take their time to get out. When the other cars hoot at them to speed them up, they shout racial abuse at the drivers of the other cars. They call the other drivers names like 'Boesman' [a derogatory term for a San person]. I often think to myself that these people are wrong to act like that, but you cannot tell them that they are wrong."

Vincent Barnes

Cricket coach Vincent Barnes used his area of expertise, sport, to explain racism.

"We have had unity in cricket for over ten years, yet we still talk about 'them' and 'us'. We still describe ourselves in the racial categories that we occupied before unity. We also find that people who have a rich heritage or a strong history of involvement in non-racial cricket are being ignored by the powers that be.

"One always hears what Graeme Pollock and Barry Richards [white former South African cricketers] did. Yet, we had our own heroes, people such as Lefty Adams and Rushdie Magiet, and nobody hears what they did, although they were fantastic players and contributed much to the sport. It is only because of skin colour that their contributions are not recognised.

"Until today, I feel that not enough has been done by the former [white] cricket union people to accept the former [black] cricket board people. If we can do that, we will be able to get rid of the 'them' and the 'us' that still pervades cricket today.

"It is not very easy to define racism, but it is something that is generally there every day. It is part of our lives. Racism is a big word, but it is about marginalisation and denying ourselves the right to be ourselves.

"I can talk about my own situation, where I am one of two coaches at Western Province. However, the newspapers only focus on the white coach. A lot of people have come to me and asked me whether I still coach because they only read about the white coach.

"In my first year of coaching Western Province, a few of the older players decided that they would make sure that I got kicked out in my first year. They decided not to cooperate with me, because of my race. At the end of the season, one of the senior players sat with me in a restaurant and apologised to me. He said that he had been part of what happened to me that season. He said what happened to me was done intentionally by members of the team.

"I knew exactly who was involved, but I have learnt that, if you are black, they will always try to hammer you, they will always try to break you down. I refused to let them break me down. I decided to stand firm. I went to my boss at Western Province and said that if he thought I could not do the job, he had to fire me. But if he fired me, he must accept the consequences. It would mean that he was accepting what those people had done to me.

"I came out of this experience a lot stronger. I decided I don't have to mix socially with the players, but they must respect my position as the coach. What has happened is that many of the white players have become close friends. My relationship with them, and with the other [white] coach, is basically open and honest. We respect each other and discuss the problems we have. We jointly find solutions."

"The majority of South Africans are living their lives in much the same way as they did under apartheid. White people still refuse to share the things they had under apartheid. At least things are easier with the younger generation. They are brought up together. They go to school together and they play sport together. But the adults remain racist. For instance, you must accept that when a black player is picked for the national side, no matter which sport, that he has to do something special. He has to score a try, he has to take wickets, or he has to score 100 runs. If he fails to do that, he will be criticised as an affirmative action player."

Leo de Souza and Obed Zilwa

Asked whether people were still racist in South Africa today, Obed Zilwa answered: "Yes, big time."

Leo da Souza said that she and Obed lived in a false sense of reality. "We have friends from different backgrounds and we live in an environment where everyone is mixed. When I visit my mother and my brothers I get a sense of reality. My friends there are all the same race and the same culture. They are so scared to venture out. No matter how many national symbols we have, we will fail if we do not get this integration thing going. White people, especially, need to be told that it is okay to venture out of their little comfort zones. They are very similar to coloured people, who stay in their little boxes.

"My mother apologised to Obed. She told him that she had been stupid and she asked him for forgiveness. But you know, ultimately, you have to forgive yourself."

One of Leo's relatives is married to a woman who is extremely racist. "She is very disrespectful towards Nelson Mandela. Every time I am there, she engages me in a discussion on racism. It hurts my mother-in-law and my father-in-law, but there is nothing they can do, because she is also a member of the family.

"The only way you are going to stop racism is when people start accepting things as they are. They have to accept that we are living in a country where there are many other races and many other cultures."

Obed added: "Most whites, when the rainbow nation came, thought 'they won't kill us'. That was their biggest fear before the 1994 elections. All the guns and ammunition were sold out just before the elections, because white people were worried about what was going to happen. Then we became the rainbow nation and everything was okay."

Leo said they still had to deal with racism on many different levels. "I still watch people's reactions when Obed is around. A white woman was standing at a bank auto-teller machine and Obed was standing behind her. I could see the tension inside her."

"The other day we had a situation where we helped someone whose car got stuck," said Obed. "I stopped to help her and she did not trust me. She kept on saying that she was from Germany and someone had gone to phone someone to help her. I said she could phone Germany from my phone. She first refused and it took me a while to convince her that she could trust me."

Khusta and Karen Jack
Khusta explained that racism was still a problem in South Africa because of certain "unnecessary compromises" that were made just after the elections in 1994. "These compromises made white people feel very comfortable and gave them the excuse to regroup in their

racist ways. There was an expectation that racism could be wiped out in South Africa, and sometimes people like me blame Nelson Mandela for encouraging racism. Not directly, but through his overzealousness on reconciliation, he allowed the gap for racists to regroup.

"Now the racists are not serious racists, like the Afrikanerweerstandsbeweging [AWB]. Those guys are not a problem to South Africa at all. The dangerous racist, the one that we need to cripple, is the one that is subtle, the one that is silently trying to say: 'They are still black and are not to be trusted. They are definitely going to mess up. They may not be messing up now, but they are going to mess up.'

"You don't get that from the Afrikaners. The Afrikaners are openly scared of losing what they have accumulated in apartheid. They are not ashamed about that. Therefore their struggle within South Africa is legitimate, as far as I am concerned.

"What worries me is the general ideological kind of differences which emanate at the level of intellectuals in this country. For instance, the debates about whether the media is racist or not and the debate by educated people about the soccer team or the cricket team or the rugby team, always linking their performance to transformation. Those things are not going to end soon."

Karen felt that racism existed on an intellectual level. "The people who perpetrated racism would be horrified if you called them racists. What they are doing they would not recognise as racism. But it is hanging onto the way things were. In Port Elizabeth, the media plays a big part in this, in hanging onto that perception."

"On the other hand," said Khusta, "I have never had it so good, in terms of safety. When I walk in the township I don't fear any more. When I see a police car, I don't think that I need to run for cover, which used to be the norm for many of us. I am talking about ordinary people, not only activists.

"I think the good news is that racism is seen as a bad thing in South Africa at the moment. Nobody who perpetrates it can stand up and say 'Yes, I did this', because it is a shame. I think it is definitely going to go. It is not a thing that we want to be associated with.

"The unfortunate thing is that black South Africans don't

understand sometimes how racist their conversations can be. They have the advantage that other people cannot understand what they are saying when they talk to each other. It is not like when two white people speak English and Afrikaans and we can pick it up. What we need to do is make black people understand racism when it happens."

Tracy-Lee Rosslind

Tracy-Lee defined racism as follows: "Racism is the way people are judged harshly on the basis of the colour of their skin. It is when people are treated differently from one another because of the colour of their skin.

"In the past, people were separated by law. Now the laws have changed, and we actually have to deal with the fact that we now have coloured, black and white neighbours. We are now thrown together and have to basically work it out. But people are still so close-minded."

Keathelia Satto

Keathelia Satto said that racism involved insulting someone on the basis of their colour. "Even if a black person insults a white person, then that is racism."

She believed racism was still a problem in South Africa. "First of all there is the issue of jobs. Sometimes, to get a job you must be white or you must be black. Also, in school, sometimes they choose the white children for sports rather than the coloured children. Often the coloured children are better at sport than the white children, but people continue to choose white people over black people. That is racist."

She said that racism was also being passed on from parents to children.

My thoughts

Roderick Blackman Ngoro, the media adviser to the former mayor of Cape Town, caused an outcry when certain comments were posted on his website. In these comments, he referred to coloureds as "drunkards" and said that Africans were "culturally superior" to coloureds. The response to Ngoro was actually more interesting than his comments and, in a sense, exposed a coloured nationalism that was emerging in the Western Cape. This was evidenced in, for instance, the comments by a group calling themselves the "Concerned Coloured Clergy", who claimed to represent 15 denominations and thousands of congregants. They threatened to advise their congregations not to vote for the ANC in local government elections if the mayor did not fire Ngoro.

Many people were offended by Ngoro's comments, including myself, but most people neglected to look at the reasons why Ngoro chose to make the comments he did – to stimulate discussion and expose what he perceived to be coloured racism. In fact, the response to Ngoro probably confirmed his assertion that racism exists within the coloured community.

Clearly the issue of racism is not being discussed enough in South African society. This could have major repercussions. Not talking about racism will not make it go away. And if it remains in the background, there will always be the potential for it to re-emerge as a major problem in the future.

CHAPTER 4
THE AFTER-EFFECTS OF APARTHEID

Blaming it on race

Just over ten years since becoming a democracy, the government and the people of South Africa still face many challenges. Chief among these are job creation, HIV/Aids and the provision of housing. Crime is also cited as a major problem in South Africa, but I believe that it is a by-product of other problems.

While I acknowledge that HIV/Aids and crime are serious issues, I rate job creation and housing as the greatest challenges facing South Africa. HIV/Aids can be contained with proper education and proper medical intervention on the part of government. Granted, this has not happened as speedily as expected, but there are positive signs that something is about to happen now that the government has at last made several billions of rands available for the fight against HIV/Aids. Crime is very much the result of factors such as poverty and unemployment. If fewer people were poor and fewer people were unemployed, I believe we would have less crime in our country.

Because of the limited resources available in South Africa, jobs and stakes in the economy are always going to be seriously contested. And that contestation will sometimes lead to all kinds of myths and accusations. One of these myths is that because of affirmative action, African and coloured people have benefited more than white people from job creation in recent years. According to an article in the *Cape Times* in November 2003, a report which was discussed at the Western Cape Growth and Development Summit indicated that only 3 out of every 100 African people in the province found work in the province between 1995 and 2002, compared with 92 out of every 100 white job seekers. Coloureds did much better than Africans, but still only 54 out of every 100 managed to find work in the province. This still leaves 46 out of every 100 without jobs.

Granted, this is the Western Cape so there are all kinds of unique dynamics at play, but I am convinced that if a national survey were done, the statistics would not be very different. This report, it seems, was partly responsible for the Western Cape provincial government announcing an ambitious plan to create 200 000 jobs in the next few years in the public and private sectors. I use the words "partly responsible" because I believe that the elections in 2004 probably played a big role in that announcement.

I have some concerns regarding this announcement. Firstly, if you announce that there are more than 500 000 people who need jobs and you announce a plan to create only 200 000 jobs, this indicates that you are prepared to live with a failure mark; 200 000 is only 40 per cent of 500 000, which is not good enough. Secondly, some of those jobs are short-term while others will only kick in over the next five years. I think this announcement, while promising in theory, will disappoint people when it comes to implementation.

I asked the people I interviewed what they regarded as South Africa's greatest challenge. The following are some excerpts from their answers.

Melanie Verwoerd

Melanie Verwoerd's opinion was that South African's main challenges involved socio-economic issues related to the legacy of apartheid.

"The other problem," she said, "is that many South Africans have such a bad image of themselves. I don't understand that. For a long time, people overseas admired us when we said we were from South Africa. Now it is almost as if we make it our duty to ensure that people don't do that any more. I find this all around me: people, mainly whites, being constantly negative and sending this message to the outside world.

Asked if this negativity was more common among English or Afrikaans-speaking whites, she replied: "It is not among all whites. There are amazing Afrikaner people who have embraced the new South Africa and the change in South Africa. In fact, surveys conducted before the 1994 elections showed that 70 per cent of English people were considering emigrating, while 70 per cent of Afrikaners felt that they would stay because they had nowhere to go. Afrikaners like me would not know where to go. There is no other place in the world for us. There are many English-speaking South Africans who still have an affinity with England or other English-speaking countries. I think that they want to keep a back door open.

"The English also whinge when they realise that they cannot go anywhere. They whinge even more than the Afrikaners. I know I am making crude generalisations and this might not be exclusive to the white community, but I cannot speak comfortably about other communities. These people who whinge use crime as an excuse for their negativity. They also privatise society in a big way. They send their children to private schools; they belong to private golf clubs on private golfing estates, where they have big walls to keep out people who don't belong. It is a real escapism from society. It says, 'We pay our taxes and we vote, but we don't engage in society beyond that.'

"I am sure that we will sort out our socio-economic problems. However, if something is going to sabotage this, it is this negativism, because it is spreading into the outside world.

"I was at a rugby match in Dublin, talking about tourism, when this guy came to me and told me that South Africa was falling apart. I said 'Not the South Africa I know' and I asked him what he was talking about. He said he had heard that people could no longer go onto the beach at Plettenberg Bay, because there were armed gangs who hijacked people, took all their clothes and left them naked on the beach. He said that this happened all the time. He had been told this by a friend from South Africa. My sister had been in Plett the previous week on holiday and had a fantastic time, so I was able to tell him that his story was not true.

"This is a simplistic example and one can probably laugh at it, but this sort of negativism is endemic. It is important, if we want to attract investors, not to show this negative perception of our country. I heard about one Irish person who was on his way to South Africa to invest big money in our country. Apparently, on his way to the airport his solicitor called and said he had just spoken to some South Africans and wanted to know whether his will was in order. Luckily he was already on the plane and so could not turn back. When he got off the plane on the other end, he was shaking with fear.

"Our country is beautiful and we have lovely products to sell. But if we give people the slightest doubt, they are not going to invest in our country.

"It is because South Africa has a black government that some white people want to believe that things are worse now than they were under apartheid."

Rhoda Kadalie

"People are beginning to say that racism is no longer the biggest issue," said Rhoda. "The South African Institute of Race Relations conducted a survey in 2001. Racism was way down on the list of priorities. People rated issues such as unemployment, poverty and crime as more important. I am not negating racism, but I am saying it is no longer our biggest problem."

On the other hand, Rhoda saw one of our greatest challenges as being the way people, especially politicians, used the race card to justify political misdemeanours such as corruption. "I have a huge problem with the way in which the struggle against racial discrimination has been minimised and diminished by people who will not accept that blacks can be corrupt," she said. "They do not believe that when you give black people power, they can become a law unto themselves and that they can turn against the very people who voted them into power.

"What I find problematic is that we have inherited a system of huge discrimination gaps between the rich and the poor. The government is not delivering to black people, who are saying that you can see the whites are still rich and nothing has changed. The government does not take responsibility for the fact that we have those huge gaps. For example, if the government decided we should not prioritise arms, but should rather prioritise issues such as job creation and unemployment and racism, then the story would be different.

"We now have a huge black economic empowerment scheme which is just a game played by black men. It is a male construct. Very few women are involved in the empowerment game.

"We have made serious mistakes around affirmative action and employment equity. We are the one country in the world with all the rules in the book around affirmative action, but we implement it wrongly. When we implement affirmative action, we redress the disadvantages suffered by blacks and women, but we do not consider merit and qualification. That's our first mistake. When we appoint blacks, we set them up for failure. We do not train them, and we do not provide them with staff development that will go a long way to assisting affirmative action.

"In Australia and Canada there are eight rules that accompany the implementation of affirmative action. These include staff development, the correct recruitment policies, correct selection policies, appointment committees, sanctions when people do wrong, rewards when people do right, the right context and atmosphere, and changing the work ethos. All of those factors are meant to assist affirmative action, but we don't have these conditions here.

"So we find that racial prejudices increase because blacks are not delivering. And blacks are not delivering because they are not educated. Apartheid was about the fact that 95 per cent of the population was denied education and skills development.

"I worked in the Human Rights Commission and the Land Commission, both case studies of affirmative action gone wrong. I can give you examples of how affirmative action has led to affirmative inaction. Trevor Manuel, our Minister of Finance, admitted in his [2002] budget speech that there was a serious lack of skills in high places in the public sector. I walk around companies and people say that they will no longer employ black people, because previous black employees could not perform. Then we ask them: 'Did you train them? Did you provide other support mechanisms?' The answer is always 'no'.

"These are the biggest challenges we face: skills development, education, job creation, the struggle against poverty, Aids, healthcare and housing. When we address these problems, then the issues of race will diminish."

Phatekile Holomisa

Phatekile Holomisa maintained that the biggest problem facing South Africa was inequity. "The majority does not have access to land and those who have access to land do not have access to the resources with which to make their land productive," he said. "For instance, in what used to be called the homelands, we have access to tribal land, but because there are no individual guarantees, we cannot put this land forward as collateral for bank loans. If you put land forward as collateral, it means that the bank can kick you out if you are unable to pay your loan. The dilemma we have is that we need land to live on and to make a living from, but we also don't want people to lose their rights to live on the land. At the same time, we need money, but before you can get money, you need to put your land up as collateral.

"The majority of our people are still poor, so this would mean that a few South Africans who have money and who are mainly white, will be in a position to take over even the 13 per cent of land that is now under occupation by blacks.

"I believe the level of poverty among blacks is due to the inequitable distribution of wealth. The crime and other issues are a result of the fact that too many people have too little while too few have too much.

"When you talk about black empowerment, this refers to a few individuals who have benefited and become like whites. They don't change that environment to ensure that as many of our people as possible can share from the wealth that they have. For instance in the big companies, even the parastatals that are headed by blacks, you find that the wages of the ordinary employees remain at the lowest level while the wages of the black leaders is continually increasing. You look at their cars, their houses and their offices, and they are becoming bigger and bigger. Yet a lot of their employees, the people for whom we are supposed to be striving, remain poor.

"In our culture, when a child obtains a certificate, for instance, the entire village celebrates because it expects to get something. One of their people has now become somebody and whatever skills he or she has are going to be used for the benefit of the people. In the early days you found that a child who was able to read or write letters, would be an asset to the entire community, because that child would write letters on behalf of the community. This is the sharing that I have talked about earlier.

"The same would apply if you were an engineer, for instance. You would want to persuade your firm to go and build roads and bridges in your community. Or if you worked for the health department, you would want to make sure that they provided a clinic in your village. You would do this because you would know that your community is looking up to you and relying on you to bring about a change in their lives. But that does not happen enough in our country."

Trevor Oosterwyk

Trevor believed that racism ranked as one of the biggest problems in our society. "If we do acknowledge this, then we are going to reduce it and its importance. And we are going to begin to say that it is not a problem in our society any more. We cannot afford to turn a blind eye. We still have to deal with racism. I think it is only white people who would like to close the agenda on the discussion of racism. I get the sense that they are tired of it. We can never get tired of it. We need to put it on the agenda many times."

Carel Boshoff

Carel Boshoff felt that all of South Africa's problems could be linked to poverty. "Many people, when you speak about poverty, would be tempted to think of one or two standard mechanisms that can be used to alleviate poverty, or they would talk about using a major economic development which, with typical market-driven stimulants, would trickle down to the poor. Or there would be a bigger involvement of government in solving this problem."

"It looks like a constructive thing to say that one must draw a distinction between poverty and a lack of resources. Poverty also has a sort of social and cultural dimension, which in the first place has to do with desire, and not with a lack of resources. This lack of resources must simply, on a human level, be dealt with by using whatever instruments a community has at its disposal, namely access to the state and to whatever development funds [are available] in the public and private sectors.

"But in this relationship between poverty and desire, one can also be critical of the market logic and of the kind of uncritical embrace of globalisation. In other words, I would be tempted to adopt a very critical view of globalisation and the setting of market values as an absolute. I would argue that one needs to look at this issue with a lot more of a community consciousness. We can learn to address this question with a focus on self care in the community and in this way address the central problem.

"I have not kept up to date with all the nuances of the HIV/Aids debate, but one cannot escape from the statement that Mr Mbeki made about the link between poverty and HIV/Aids. Whatever the medical arguments involved, everything has to do with poverty. Many of South Africa's problems have everything to do with poverty."

Wilmot James
Wilmot James regarded our greatest challenges as HIV/Aids and poverty.

"Poverty is about the exclusion of resources and assets and it has a racial structure to it," he said. "My sense is that where we used to have apartheid before, we probably have economic apartheid nowadays.

"For instance, my children go to former Model C schools and at the one school the fees have risen by about 60 per cent in the last three years. That is another way in which white people use economic means to exclude essentially black people. For me, that is a form of economic apartheid. I am sure it is deliberate because often people would want to send their children to the best schools and, if they have the resources to pay for it, this is what happens. But the consequence is that they are putting public and private schooling in the reach of only the wealthy in our society. They have exploited the fact that black people might not necessarily have access to the kind of money to afford to send their children to these schools.

"I think economic power in South Africa will remain in white hands for a long time to come. Combine this with the fact that the state will be in black hands for a long time to come, and you have an ongoing battle, at least for the next 20 years, as long as resources in society are not distributed equally."

Naledi Pandor

The biggest problem in South Africa, according to Naledi Pandor, was the fact that "most of the poor are black and most whites are unable to understand that they have to play a role in changing this."

Kenny and Sielie Nolan

Kenny Nolan cited unemployment as a major problem. "More and more people are at home. I have worked for many, many years and this is the first time that I find myself at home, without work."

Sielie commented on the importance of creating jobs, and on the issue of gangsterism. "We want to be able to give our children the best so that they can be better children. We want to give them education, and in this way, we could do away with gangsterism. However, because of poverty, gangsterism thrives in our communities. When parents are unable to give their children what they need, the children will look for these things elsewhere. This is how gangsterism develops. This is our biggest problem."

Sielie said she did not that believe racism was still the biggest problem in South Africa. "The new government has made many changes, for instance in education, and the day hospitals and other hospitals are now free. This helps people like us who are underprivileged. We don't pay a lot of money at the hospitals any more. That is a positive thing done by the government."

Vincent Barnes

Vincent Barnes saw our country's greatest challenge as learning to accept each other as human beings, despite our different pigmentation. "People just generally struggle to accept that people of colour can be talented, not only in sport, but also in the commercial and professional arenas. People will always make excuses when black people do well. They will say things like 'He's such a skilful bowler, but ...' There always has to be a 'but'.

"I think it is going to take a long time for people to accept that all of us are human beings. This is a major problem in our society."

Athena Sotomi

When I interviewed her, Athena Sotomi felt that HIV/Aids was a bigger problem than racism. "However," she said, "racism might still be the biggest problem for some South Africans. Violence against women and children would probably come a close second. I can see from my voluntary work that there are many people from different cultural backgrounds working together very hard to stop that kind of thing. In this environment, race is no longer an issue.

"I don't think racism will ever go away. I suppose it is how one manages it."

Leo de Souza and Obed Zilwa

"We still have so many things that are dividing us, such as railway lines and councils that still define us as blacks, as whites or as coloureds," said Leo.

She felt that while we had come a long way as a society, there were still many problems. "In the past, we would not have been able to live together as a family. We can also now register our child with a common identity number. We have a fantastic Constitution and we were going to have this wonderful democracy; we were going to have a human rights culture and build on that. But we are losing the plot somewhat. However, I think these are growing pains. It is important that we continue to have respect for each other. Racism has the potential to make us lose respect for each other.

"The important thing to remember is that it is no longer important whether you are a white South African or a black South African. South Africans have to face their challenges as one.

"I saw a white *dominee* [priest] preaching about the hurt that Wouter Basson caused to black people. He burst into tears and said he could not forgive himself. This is positive, but we still need to do a lot more to bring all our people together and to create a better understanding among them."

"Another area where things have to change is in housing," added Obed. "Until there is one housing list in South Africa, racism is still going to be a problem. Still today, white people wait for a house in Goodwood, coloured people wait for a house in Manenberg, and African people have to go to Gugulethu. If a white person can't afford a house in Goodwood and there is a house available in Khayelitsha, he should be able to take that house."

Leo agreed. "The situation with housing at the moment is that when they build houses in coloured or African areas, they will only house coloured or African people, because white people would not want to live there. What Obed is talking about is a compromise, which only comes from black people. It is not a compromise coming from white people.

"I think our leadership has done much to bring about change in different aspects of life, from local government, to provincial government and national government. But you have to bear in mind that, in everything you do, your aim must be to equalise society.

"Maybe, in some ways, we moved too fast and did not really discuss these issues properly."

Khusta and Karen Jack

"Unemployment is at the root of many of the other problems we have," stated Khusta. "As an experiment, I have taken a person who has been sitting there, unemployed and morally depressed, and given him or her a job. Within a short space of time, I have seen how that person transforms into a responsible citizen.

"I believe we will solve a lot of our problems if we are able to create jobs for our people."

Tracy-Lee Rosslind

"Racism is still one of our biggest problems," said Tracy-Lee Rosslind. "Everything else stems from racism. Crime is a big problem, and rape is a big problem. But I believe these crimes have their roots in racism. People were forced into an area that could not even hold the amount of people that were living there. And if you do not have bread and you are starving, what can you do? I am not justifying crime at all, but I am saying that it does stem from somewhere. It did not magically appear. I believe it stemmed from racism, and from the policy of segregation. We need to see that racism is a problem and it is getting worse and worse."

Keathelia Satto

Keathelia Satto first said racism was our biggest problem, and then changed her mind. "Actually, I think poverty is our biggest problem. There are just so many homeless people out there. We need to create more jobs."

My thoughts

Ten years ago racism was the biggest problem in South Africa. The Nationalist Party government used the system of apartheid to divide and rule the majority of South Africans and to ensure that white people received most of the political and economic privileges in our country.

Today, South Africa has a democratic, mainly black government for the first time, but it is evident, for the next few generations at least, this country will continue to suffer from the effects of apartheid.

Unemployment is still a major problem, especially among the black majority. Essentially, despite the government's steps to deal with the inequalities of the past through affirmative action and black economic empowerment, the majority of black people still live in sub-economic townships, often in overcrowded conditions, while the majority of whites still live in reasonable comfort.

While different people identify different issues as being our greatest challenge, the legacy of apartheid will always underpin our society.

And while poverty and job creation are clearly two of our major problems, they are accompanied by a host of other problems. Crime is one of them. Housing is another. The housing problem is a complex and expensive one to fix. It is not as straightforward as the government simply providing houses for all those without. Government needs to inculcate a culture of payment for services, including housing. Yet how does one pay for housing if one is poor or unemployed?

When Joe Slovo was our first democratic Housing Minister, the aim was to encourage home-ownership among all South Africans. However, recently it appears that government is reviewing this stance and thinking about reverting to a situation where a significant number of people will be renting. This is especially true of the N2 Gateway development in the Western Cape, which will be providing tens of thousands of rental houses to the poorest parts of our community.

The fact that the government is reviewing its position on housing sales as opposed to rentals is an indication that their present policy is probably not working. In a country such as South Africa, where there is so much unemployment and poverty, it is highly unlikely that the majority of people will be able to afford to buy their houses. Yet, it remains the responsibility of government to see that its citizens are housed (remember the Freedom Charter phrase: "There shall be houses, security and comfort"). Perhaps there is an opportunity for government to build houses for its citizens while creating jobs for the millions of unemployed, not unlike what President Franklin D. Roosevelt did in the United States during the Great Depression, when he used unemployed people to build roads and national parks, amongst other things.

Crime also has its roots in poverty. It is easy for someone who is relatively well-off to philosophise about crime, but when one is poor and has a family to feed one could be tempted to turn to crime. Of course, crime can also be linked apartheid, although one wants to be careful not to blame apartheid for everything. Nevertheless, apartheid made people live in dormitory townships where gangsterism reigned supreme and where drug lords were often seen as saviours of their communities. In fact, in some communities, drug dealers were among the most prominent providers of employment, particularly after 1994.

Another problem facing South Africa today is HIV/Aids, which is decimating large portions of our population. The government has been slow to respond to calls to supply anti-retrovirals to everyone with HIV, but lately there seems to have been movement on this issue. The reality is that if we do not respond appropriately to HIV/Aids, we will lose large chunks of our population, and many people who should be helping to grow the economy.

In conclusion, I would point out that the aim of this chapter was to look at some of the major problems facing our society, although South Africa is doing amazingly well in several areas. But as is evident from this chapter, there is still a lot of work to be done. I don't think anybody expected us to fix all our problems in a decade, but it is important to identify them so that we know what needs to be addressed.

Vincent Barnes

Carel Boshoff IV

Phatekile Holomisa

Obed Zilwa and Leo de Souza

Wilmot James

Rhoda Kadalie

Kenny and Sielie Nolan

Trevor Oosterwyk

Naledi Pandor

Tracy-Lee Rosslind

Keathelia Satto

Athena and Manny Sotomi

Melanie Verwoerd

Khusta and Karen Jack
Themba and Kayla Jack

Ryland Fisher

CHAPTER 5
IS RACISM A SOUTH AFRICAN PROBLEM?

A comparison with the United States

The American Dream

South Africans have always been fascinated by America, although most will only admit this reluctantly. Who cannot be fascinated by the world's largest economy, the world's primary supplier of movies and the world's biggest music industry? In contrast, most Americans have no idea where South Africa is, or that it is, in fact, the name of a country and not a geographic part of the African continent. Yet when you mention racism or apartheid there is a flicker of recognition among some Americans, particularly African-Americans. Indeed, some Americans are fascinated by South Africa. Part of this fascination stems from the fact that South Africa appears to have dealt with or is dealing with racism in a way that could set an example to the rest of the world.

Of course, one of the main reasons for the apartheid government agreeing to talks with the ANC in the early nineties was because of the pressure put on them by people in the United States and other countries who forcefully protested against apartheid. This isolation of the apartheid government by people and governments throughout the world forced the apartheid government to re-evaluate its strategies and to begin the talks that set South Africa on the road to becoming a democracy.

It is therefore ironic that in just over ten years South Africa seems to have made much more progress in dealing with race and racism than a country like America, which has been dealing with these issues in a so-called liberated manner for many decades.

One of the key differences between South Africa and America is that South Africa has a black majority, while America has a black minority. South Africa's black majority can use its political power to force racial issues to the top of the political agenda. In the United States, black people can easily be dismissed because they have little political power. Yes, they can vote, but that means nothing if they cannot muster sufficient votes to support them on certain issues, such as racism.

Perhaps another key difference is the way South Africans and Americans respond to issues. South Africans are used to extreme responses, such as protest marches (which can sometimes turn violent), mass meetings and consumer boycotts. The Americans use intellectual debate and the power of the pen much more than South Africans do.

Perhaps if, as some people predict, the demography of the United States were to change over the next few decades and white people were no longer the majority, then racism would become a white issue and therefore an important issue. Perhaps then something would finally be done about racism in the United States.

In this chapter, I begin by looking at some of the differences between South Africa and two American cities, Atlanta and Chicago. I realise that these two cities are not representative of the entire United States, and that things might be very different in other American cities, but as I have said, this book is not intended to be conclusive. In the interviews, I explore some comparisons between South Africa and other countries.

Atlanta
Atlanta promotes itself as the city too busy to hate. "It might be too busy to care," said Lynn Huntley, president of the Southern Education Fund. Huntley said that middle- and upper-class African-Americans in Atlanta were too preoccupied with achieving success to put anything back into the community. "It seems as if they have formed this

conspiracy of silence with the white community, based on a shared economic interest and economic privileges."

Huntley said that white people had moved out of the city centre many years ago to avoid black people. However, many of them were beginning to return because they wanted to be near their places of work. They were moving back into areas that had been historically black, at least for the past few decades.

Professor Laurence P. Jackson of Emory University took me on a tour of Atlanta and showed me the differences between black and white areas. The black areas had markedly smaller homes, many with fences and burglar bars, unlike the traditional white neighbourhoods where houses had minimal security. He showed me streets that had been given more than one name. The reason for this, he explained, was that white people did not want to live on the same street as black people, so they would change the name of the part of the street in which they lived.

Nathan McCall, a journalism professor at Emory University and author of the best-selling book *Makes Me Wanna Holler*, said that Atlanta was often described as a "Black Mecca". "It is known as one of the places in America with the highest concentration of high-earning blacks in the country. This could create the illusion that we do not have racial problems in this city."

During the time I was in Atlanta, a prominent incident involving racism took place at Emory University, when an anthropology professor used the phrase "like six niggers in a woodpile" at a function of the Department of Anthropology. The remark was heard by several faculty members, but only one, an African-American junior professor, filed a formal complaint about it. The other faculty members, who were all white, remained silent.

Around the same time there was an incident in South Africa involving a black teenage girl at Edgemead High School who was apparently attacked by a fellow learner – a white girl. The attacker was reportedly helped by her mother and white boyfriend. The details of this incident were unfortunately not contested in court because the parties reached an out-of-court settlement. However, it was assumed that the black girl was the victim, although it was possible that she could have been the perpetrator. This assumption exposed the racial stereotyping characteristic of South Africans.

The two incidents, and the responses to them in South Africa and the United States, highlighted some of the differences between the two countries.

In South Africa, the response to the incident at Edgemead High was a public campaign against racism, spearheaded by the ANC branch in the area, which no doubt had one eye on the elections that were coming up in the following year. It also involved placard protests outside the school.

The American response took the form a "town hall" meeting where the university's new president, Dr James Wagner, tried to convince a mainly black audience that he was committed to diversity; op-ed articles to newspapers, and letters from "concerned students and faculty members" to the university president. Part of this response was prompted by the reaction of some white academics who seemed to believe that it should be acceptable for academics to make racial statements. They argued that this was part of academic freedom.

The main difference between the South African and American responses was that in the United States they talked about the incident, whereas the South Africans simply jumped to conclusions.

What the incidents had in common was that they both demonstrated one of the major problems with racism: it is seen as a black problem. And therefore it is not prioritised. This is especially true in a place like the United States, where whites, for the time being at least, still form the majority of the population.

Dr Wagner, in his initial comments, tried to skirt around the issue, using terms such as "cultural insensitivity" instead of "racism". He also spoke against a recommendation that the entire faculty of Emory, who were mainly white, be put through diversity training. By the end of the meeting, however, he was using the term "racism" and considering the need for the faculty to be made aware of diversity issues, although not necessarily through training.

The main concern that the incident at Emory highlights for me is that in a place like the United States, or anywhere where blacks are a minority, there is always a danger of marginalisation. And where this is the case, it becomes all too easy to write off complaints about racism as the being work of "angry blacks".

Chicago

Chicago reminded me a bit of Cape Town. Built on the Chicago River and Lake Michigan, one of the biggest lakes in the United States, it has the distinctive feel of a coastal city. But the similarity with Cape Town does not end there. I remember walking through the streets of Chicago and searching in vain for black faces, but seeing at most a handful. I have walked through parts of Cape Town, too, and been amazed that I could see no black – particularly African – people.

Chicago, I later discovered, is divided into white, black, Hispanic and even Chinese areas. Most people I spoke to described Chicago as "the most racist city in the United States".

"Not so," said Alex Kotlowitz, award-winning author of books such as *There Are No Children Here* and *The Other Side of the River*. "I would rather describe it as the most segregated city in the United States. Racism has certain undertones which are not necessarily present in Chicago."

Kotlowitz describes himself as "something of a fan of Chicago's first black mayor, Harold Washington". Kotlowitz said that when Washington was elected mayor in the early 1980s, there was a lot of racism in that campaign. "Washington won the democratic primaries and that is normally enough for anyone to become mayor. However, many white Democrats decided to support the Republicans against Washington. When Washington won, the whites, who had the majority of council, prevented him from doing anything. It was ugly."

Harold Washington was mayor from 1983 until 1987. He was elected for a second term, but died in office.

Kotlowitz said that when it came to replacing Washington, the largely white council had to choose someone. The black people arranged a march on the city hall in protest, forcing the white councillors to choose a black mayor. "They chose Eugene Sawyer, a black man who supported the white agenda. When they announced his election, people threw dollars at him to indicate that he had sold out his people."

While Kotlowitz denied that Chicago was racist, he said that there were many indications that blacks were still suffering because of segregation. "The high rises are being torn down now, but their effects are still felt today. You can go down to any country court house and you will not find any white people there. Our county jail houses close to 10 000 people. It is the biggest in the country. Yet it is filled with mainly black prisoners. There are also no white faces at juvenile court."

Kotlowitz pointed out an irony that had become apparent since the city began desegregating. "Black businesses used to thrive in the old days. Since segregation was outlawed, black businesses have fallen apart as black people have begun to support businesses in white areas."

David Protess, a professor at the Medill School of Journalism at Northwestern University in Evanston, Chicago, said that until World War II, white ethnic groups, in coalition, had run Chicago. "They knew how to divide up power between them. Anton Cermack, who was mayor in the 1930s, founded a political machine based on ethnic politics. These ethnics were held together by what they could get out of the system, such as housing and related services. There were no major political issues," he said.

"After World War II, a large black population arrived from the South. Their numbers swelled between 1945 and the late 1950s. However, the political machine in Chicago was not prepared to accommodate them. The white ethnic groups all had one thing in common: they hated blacks.

"The mayor at the time, Richard J. Daley, the father of Chicago's present mayor, decided to segregate blacks and whites. He built large high-rise public housing projects 3 to 15 miles outside the city on the south side. Segregation also occurred on the west side of the city. This was politically significant, because in other cities, political bosses and political machinery was falling apart.

"Mayor Daley won white votes by keeping blacks out of the city. It occurred over two decades, so journalists never saw it and never reported on it. Daley's second strategy was to give blacks favours in the style of the old political machine, such as turkey on Thanksgiving Day, public housing and welfare cheques. Daley made sure that his people delivered welfare cheques, even though the cheques came from the country government.

"In exchange for having their survival needs met, blacks voted for their own oppressor, Richard Daley. Daley was mayor for 23 years, from 1953 until 1976."

Protess said that Chicago's new racism was embodied in the new mayor, Richard M. Daley, the son of the former mayor. "He seems to be embracing liberal causes, including the black community. However, only the black upper and middle classes are benefiting. He has built malls, townhouses and condos, and some public housing in white areas. There remains tremendous antagonism between whites and the black lower classes.

"The only exception was when Harold Washington was mayor in the 1980s. He was Chicago's first black mayor. He died while in office and was replaced by Eugene Sawyer, a black mayor who was in favour of the white power structure. Washington was not in favour of the white power structure."

Protess said the fastest growing group in Chicago was the Latinos, mainly Mexican immigrants, and that they were set to displace African-Americans as the largest minority.

The media is normally a good indicator of transformation. I attended a page-one meeting (where some of the most important decisions regarding content are made) at the *Chicago Tribune*, the biggest newspaper in the city. I was surprised that there were no blacks at the meeting, and only a few women, who were also white. I found it disturbing that there were no black people involved in deciding what a target market consisting of mixed races should read.

I asked my interviewees whether they felt South Africa was different to most other countries in the world with regards to racism. Most had travelled to other parts of the world.

Wilmot James
Wilmot James had been involved in a group dealing with racism in America, Brazil and South Africa. I asked him about his experiences within that group.

"It was a fascinating group," said Wilmot. "The Brazilians have not even begun to tackle the issue of race yet, because of the power of the mythology of non-racialism in their country. The fact is that most Afro-Brazilians are at the bottom of the Brazilian pile. They have only recently begun to discuss this.

"In the United States, it's a different story because you are dealing with a black minority and a white majority. So there it is all about civil rights and access. It is not about more revolutionary things like land redistribution.

"We have quite a different story here. We are fairly far advanced in terms of the discussion. The power distribution is highly beneficial. But you must remember that we have had a negotiated deal, where the deal was that white people could keep property and assets, and accumulation remained as it was, without any radical means of distribution built into it. So everything that changes on the economic front is an evolution, piece by piece.

"The US can teach us a lot about how to use the law to make that possible. We are quite inexperienced on that level. The Brazilians can teach us a lot about how to use cultural assets like art and culture to really forge an identity that's fantastic."

Rhoda Kadalie
Rhoda Kadalie's view was that South Africa differed to most other countries in the world with regards to racism.

"It is different because we have inculcated racial domination to such an extent that our language is imbued with racism and we don't even know it. Racist language is subtle and it pervades the workplace and everywhere we go. Often people don't mean to be racist, but they are racist. I don't judge people for that. It is part of a system that we have become used to. I have friends from places such as Sweden and the rest of Europe who come to conferences here and ask me whether we are just used to this kind of language."

Rhoda recalled a few instances involving racist language. "I was married to a white man and black people would come to my house and ask to see the 'madam'. Those people aren't racist. They are just conditioned that in a household where there is a white man, the wife must be white. I would fetch my daughter at school and the kids would tell her that 'your maid is looking for you'. When she tells them that it is not her maid, but her mother, they say, 'Oh, but your father is white.'

"One has to contend with these forms of racism all the time. It is part of our language. Even those of us who were in the struggle accord a different attention to different people, and we do it unwittingly. The very people who practised non-racialism would treat Clem Sunter [a white analyst linked to the Anglo-American Corporation] differently to Rhoda Kadalie in a public meeting, and they would treat Howard Barrel [a white former editor of the *Mail & Guardian*] differently to Ryland Fisher in a journalist meeting.

"South Africa is also different because we now have constitutional laws that guarantee equality. However, we have imbued our behaviour, our cultural interaction and language with racist behaviour that we are often unconscious about. A lot of it is implicit.

"What I like about the new South Africa, and what I liked about being on the Human Rights Commission, is that ordinary people are now beginning to know their rights, understanding them and acting in terms of them.

"An ordinary member of the working class, a domestic worker, will phone me up and tell me that her 'madam' has discriminated against her. There was a black woman who worked for a medical company where a doctor's wallet got lost and he immediately accused her of stealing it. Security guards came in and they strip-searched her to look for this wallet. But this woman came to me because she knew her rights. It is empowering when people know their rights and act on them. This is what I find encouraging about South Africa today."

Phatekile Holomisa

"You could say that other countries are fortunate because they are almost homogenous; there is more equality. In other countries, if the people are poor, they are all poor. If there is some kind of prosperity, everyone moves at more or less the same rate. But here we have this history of an unequal distribution of wealth. We also have a situation where the colonisers, the oppressors, are in the minority, and yet they have instilled their values in the education system and they continue to horde the wealth of the country to themselves, despite our political liberation.

"This is the situation all over the world where there are people of European descent. In places such as Australia, Canada or America, they came and dispossessed the inhabitants of the land. And they continue to dominate the indigenous people.

"At the same time we are fortunate in that we used the education and training that was available to us, even if only to a limited extent, to be able to understand their way of thinking and their culture, and therefore to enable us to come up with systems that are intended to overcome the obstacles brought about by our history."

Carel Boshoff

Carel Bosshoff said he was not a world traveller and did not feel qualified to speak about racism in other countries.

"However, I think we are different in the sense that we had a racially-based system until fairly recently. But one has to consider that this was only for a limited period, and that as time goes by, this period will seem even shorter.

"I suspect that we are not very different to other countries. Some of the crudest racist expressions I have heard were not made in South Africa or by South Africans. So in that sense, I don't think South Africa is in a totally different position to other countries."

Melanie Verwoerd

Melanie Verwoerd claimed that racism had become more of an issue in many countries, and especially in those that she had visited.

"People in these countries wouldn't necessary call it racism, but they will talk about xenophobia. This is certainly the case in Ireland, where I spent a lot of time, and in England and America.

"There are deeper issues that people throughout the world have to deal with, such as the fear of people who are different to them, especially in countries which are in transition. The whole debate over immigrants, for instance, is big."

Trevor Oosterwyk

Trevor Oosterwyk reckoned South Africa was similar to other countries who were dealing with multicultural problems, "even European countries such as England".

"Most of the world is dealing with the issue of different kinds of cultural groups living in the same cities," he said. "I think we are different in that we have this chance to create a society that is different. We have the opportunity to show that we can break the back of racism and establish an equitable society were race is not important. By saying that we have this opportunity does not mean that everybody else did not have this opportunity. Because we come out of years of apartheid, we have the moral high ground. We resolved much of the conflict [around apartheid] in a way that was not expected and that provided us with an opportunity to speak about racism and other issues in our society.

"Of course, we have to realise that there is always this threat of a white backlash. If we don't deal with it, it is going to be a problem. But we have an opportunity to deal with it in a different way, and learn from the experience of, for instance, the people in America."

Vincent Barnes

Vincent said he was surprised to encounter more racism in England and Scotland than he'd experienced in mid-1980s South Africa.

"Yes, we had apartheid and separate development and everything was still totally separate in South Africa, but I would be subjected to racial abuse openly in the streets in England and Scotland. That never really happened in South Africa," he said.

"The racism in Scotland was particularly bad. Here people think in racial terms, but they will not necessarily say what they are thinking.

"I got an opportunity to play in Scotland through an organiser in

Johannesburg. Because my name is Vincent Barnes and not, for instance, Imran Khan, they did not know what they were going to get. There was tension from the minute I got off the plane and this guy came to meet me. I did not know what was going on. He took me to the clubhouse and the minute he introduced me, there was a kind of hush. It was crazy.

"They only really started to talk to me a few weeks later. The chairman and the club captain then told me that when I walked in on the first day, they thought I was a Pakistani and the last person they wanted was a Pakistani. It took a hell of a long time to convince them I am a Christian and I live in South Africa. I am South African and a Christian and I am not Pakistani, you know."

Athena and Manny Sotomi

"The first thing most people throughout the world talk about is race. Racism exists everywhere. There is racism in the caste system [in India and elsewhere], and there is even racism within the black culture. People want to know if you are Xhosa, or from Mozambique or Nigeria," said Manny.

"There are so many people who leave South Africa, and particularly Cape Town, for places such as Australia, New Zealand, the United States and Britain. Many of them leave for racist reasons, such as fear of a black government, and have to come back with their tails between their legs when they discover that things in those other countries are not better, but actually worse than in South Africa.

"But people are people and people make countries. South Africans of all races are friendlier than the people in most other countries I have visited. Maybe South Africans are a bit more ignorant than people in most other countries."

Athena intervened. "It depends on which perspective you are coming from. From a racial perspective, I think South Africans are a bit more paranoid about race than people from other countries. South Africans are awakening from a long sleep that was caused by apartheid, when we were cut off from the rest of the world, when we had sanctions and other things. We are now suddenly discovering that there is a whole big world out there."

Leo de Souza and Obed Zilwa

"We still have a long way to go, but at least we are dealing with racism," said Leo. "America, for instance, has not dealt with their race issue. Even the UK has not dealt with it. We still have a lot of passion and we are still young enough as a country to do something about racism. It seems like countries such as America and the UK have lost their passion. It seems to me that we are ahead in our approach to these issues. For instance, we may be more advanced than Americans in terms of human relations.

"However, when it comes to socio-economic problems in South Africa, we have many. One of our biggest problems is that many people are poor. And the issue of race is always going to have to be addressed in terms of this poverty."

Obed added that most South Africans were proud to be South Africans, even those who were poor.

Khusta and Karen Jack

"I have been very impressed with England," said Khusta. "The English have the right attitude towards racism. In England, if the politicians are arguing about racism, none of them would take the side that perpetuates racism. They will always denounce racism.

"Of course they have their problems, but Britain, in my opinion, is more intolerant of racism than most other countries."

Tracy-Lee Rosslind

Tracy-Lee Rosslind, despite her youth, had been to several countries overseas, including Australia, Singapore and Malaysia.

"As far as Australia goes, I have to say that we are better," she said. "In South Africa, even though there is racism, you can still see us all walking down the same road together. In Australia, my mother ran up to a black woman on the station in excitement, because all you see there are white people.

"We moved into a house in Australia and there were just white people. It was myself, my sister, my mother and my father and they [the white people] said they had never seen so many blacks in one place before. So I do feel South Africa is a bit further ahead."

My thoughts

Because South Africa has only recently emerged from legalised apartheid, the memory of institutionalised racism is still fresh in our minds. The way we defeated legalised racism, without significant bloodshed, is one of the lessons that South Africa can share with the world. When it comes to dealing with race and racism, South Africa can play a moral role by setting an example to the international community.

Another difference between South Africa and many other countries is that South Africa has been blessed with several leaders who grew up opposing apartheid and racism, and as a consequence, non-racialism has been on the country's agenda for many years. And as Wilmot James pointed out, South Africa has a black majority, whereas many countries dealing with racism, such as the United States, have a black minority. Having a black majority means that black people can make the rules governing society and thus they can make the outlawing of racism a key priority.

It is clear to me that we are trying to deal with racism, while in many other countries it is being swept under the carpet. The only way to deal with racism is to confront it head on. Otherwise, it will always be with us.

CHAPTER 6
XENOPHOBIA

'They are coming to take our jobs'

In the struggle days, the ANC and other liberation movements such as the Pan Africanist Congress (PAC) depended on other African countries for support in the fight for freedom. This support ranged from housing ANC and PAC members who had gone into exile, to assisting with their education.

During the apartheid years, the ANC set up its headquarters in Lusaka, Zambia. They established a school, the Solomon Mahlangu Freedom College, in Mazimbu, Tanzania. They also fought alongside the South West African People's Organisation (Swapo) in Namibia, Frelimo in Mozambique, and the Popular Movement for the Liberation of Angola (MPLA) in Angola.

When apartheid ended, and the ANC became the government of a newly democratic South Africa, it was expected that all Africans, especially those from the countries that had actively supported the anti-apartheid struggle, would be able to share in the joy of the new democracy.

But this has not happened, because some South Africans feel threatened by immigrants from other African countries. They claim that these "foreigners" come to South Africa to take away jobs from the locals. They argue that there are too few jobs for South Africans as it is. Yet in reality, people from other African countries seldom take away jobs from locals. In fact, many immigrants have started up businesses in South Africa and have actually created jobs for locals.

There has also been a negative response to African-Americans who come to South Africa to assist in rebuilding the country and its economy, again due to fear of jobs being taken away from South Africans.

The responses from local Africans have been violent at times, fuelled in part by xenophobic reports in the media about the influx of people from Nigeria and other countries. The image often portrayed is that these people are drug dealers and gangsters. There have been reports of people being beaten up or thrown off trains because they were foreign, especially in the Gauteng area.

My concern is that government, in not creating a proper awareness of xenophobia, may be knowingly or unknowingly inciting people who are acting violently against foreign Africans. In the past, government has claimed increasing reports of "positive correlations" between illegal immigration and crimes such as prostitution, drug abuse, money laundering, sale of counterfeit goods, illegal arms trafficking and car hijackings for cross-border markets.

In contrast, during apartheid the government encouraged white people to immigrate. The perception was that these workers were skilled and therefore an asset to South Africa. Yet despite the fact that many of the African immigrants are equally skilled, they are not welcomed in the same way. Even today, there is not much response from black South Africans towards white immigrants. It seems that black South Africans do not view them as competition.

I asked the people I interviewed why there is so much xenophobia in South Africa and how we could fight it.

Athena and Manny Sotomi

Manny Sotomi, whose parents are from Nigeria, said he had not personally experienced much xenophobia. "But I have seen a lot of it. I have been working in a township and whenever it rears its head, I tend to find that the leadership nips it in the bud. But I know that xenophobia exists. It is there. I know it is there.

"I had an incident once when I drove my Audi A4 to a council meeting in Khayelitsha. One person who used to serve on the council said: 'All these people come here and they drive these nice cars and stuff life that.' He asked me whether I would have driven a car like that if I had stayed in Nigeria. I told him that I actually did not come from Nigeria. I lived in Britain. But if I was in Nigeria, I would have had the choice of 14 cars, including a Porsche and a Range Rover, because my father collected cars. He looked at me and kept quiet after that.

"Another experience of xenophobia was when somebody from Khayelitsha reported me to the Department of Home Affairs as an illegal alien. They actually came to my office. I was very pissed off with them. I shouldn't have been, but I was. At the time, I was working with the Department of Home Affairs to get them new offices in the CBD development in Khayelitsha. They had a little garage and you would have hundreds of people registering at this office. I thought they were coming to discuss this development. The one man asked me a question in Xhosa and I told him I didn't speak Xhosa. He asked me where I was from and I asked what he wanted. He then said that somebody had called them to tell them that I was an illegal alien. I had to inform them that I was actually invited to become a resident by the South African government. Of course, they would not renew my work permit unless I became a permanent resident. I got very upset.

"So, I have had some experience of xenophobia, though nothing major, but I have seen it happening and we see it in the news – about people getting thrown off trains and killed. It is terrible."

Athena said she became a victim of xenophobia in a roundabout way. "Wherever I am working, Manny will phone me at work at some stage and people will say 'Oh, is your husband American?' and I will say 'He is Nigerian'. Suddenly they will back off and there will be silence. Sometimes somebody will make a crack about Nigerians being drug dealers and I do not tolerate that.

Manny said he was very proud to be Nigerian, because his parents are Nigerian. "However, I am also a naturalised South African. There are times now when I actually just tell people that I am a South African. Before I became a South African, I would speak to people at a function and they would ask me where I was from. When I'd say I was from Nigeria, that would just kill the conversation. It's not everybody that does this, though. It is really a minority."

Athena added: "It's across the board. It does not just come from a particular class of people. The other thing that happens is that when people hear my husband is from Nigeria, they want to know whether he is tall and whether he wears flowing robes."

"Well, I'm not tall," said Manny, "but I do wear flowing robes from time to time."

"Sometimes when we go out," joked Athena, "we both end up wearing dresses."

Naledi Pandor

"As African people, we should be able to travel quite freely," said Naledi Pandor. "Many of us were supported by African countries when we were outside the country.

"If there are people in our country who go around looking for Africans from foreign countries and attacking them, that is a criminal act and they must be dealt with harshly. We need to appreciate diversity beyond our borders as South African people. Maybe as political leaders we should say more about accepting that we are a multiplicity of people on the continent, and that we should be able to accept each other.

"I get my hair done at a hairdresser owned by a Ghanaian and the young ladies who braid my hair are French-speaking Congolese. The young men who do the setting of my hair are Xhosa-speaking and they are from Gugulethu. There's a young woman who is very good with weaving and she's Kenyan. So in my hairdresser there is real diversity of Africans. I haven't seen them fighting and I've been going there for a few years.

"I have a difficulty, sometimes, with the impression that there's a huge amount of xenophobia. I might be wrong in wanting to draw from my own experience, but I have been trying to understand the sense and nature of the xenophobia I read so much about in the newspapers. Is it that we make some incidents much larger than they are, or is it that we are having constant attacks on Africans in our communities? I don't know the answer but certainly we must learn to live with a range of people. That's part of diversity management."

Phatekile Holomisa

Phatekile Holomisa believed that people should make a living in their own countries. "It is necessary for people to exchange their views and their cultures, but this has to be done in a regulated manner," he said. "You can't just allow people who feel like coming to a country to come in. There must be a regulated immigration system. People tend to put emphasis on the fact that many of our people involved in the liberation struggle found succour in other countries. They were treated relatively humanely in these countries, but that was because of circumstances here in South Africa.

"During the struggle, South Africans did not just go into these other countries any way they wanted to. There was an arrangement between those governments and the liberation movement to ensure that people could come in. There was a need for support to be given.

"Some people are now coming into South Africa because of oppressive conditions in their countries caused by mismanagement of the affairs of those countries, and often resulting in violence.

"What needs to happen is for our government to work with our counterparts in the SADC [Southern African Development Community] and other international forums to make sure that the economic and political systems in those countries are sound. If this happens, it will not be necessary for people to flee their countries as refugees.

"Many people in South Africa are poor and unemployed, and many of the people who come from other countries come here in search of a greener pasture. It is important that people are able to do that, but it must be regulated. They must not come in illegally. Some of them get employed on farms which are supposed to employ our own people. They get employed because they are desperate, and they are prepared to be overworked and underpaid. That creates resentment among South Africans.

"It is not just a simple matter of xenophobia. We can't forever be indebted to other countries. The truth of the matter is that some of these countries resented the presence of our people in their territories. They just tolerated us because apartheid was so disgusting that no one would openly do things that could be seen to be supporting apartheid."

Khusta and Karen Jack

Khusta said: "I believe that our people want to pass on to others the negative outcome of their own experience.

"Our people believe that Africans are inferior. This country has an equal number of foreigners from Europe and from Africa. Africans have started moving here in the years since we became a democracy, but there are many Europeans who came to this country before then, and many of them were even illegal. But nobody cares about that and they are not exposed when they come to work here.

"Because of apartheid, blacks in South Africa had no connection with people from other African countries, such as Zimbabwe. So when Africans come to our country, they are exposed. They don't have friends to introduce them to anybody and they end up becoming a very visible community of poor people. And they are also seen to crowd in on the limited resources that we have in our country. It then becomes an economic battle. What makes it worse is that many of these Africans are much better educated than many of our people in South Africa.

"I don't think the government can be blamed for everything that people do. I think, however, that government needs to do more in terms of educating people that these people are people just like us. Also, the phenomenon of migration between countries can even lead to economic growth."

Karen Jack felt that there was racism in xenophobia. "There are people here who come from America and England, and there is no xenophobia against them. It seems it is just an African, a black, thing."

Khusta suggested that xenophobia could be addressed through education and social interaction. "Recently there was a school from Uganda that was touring South Africa and they stayed in Soweto. This kind of thing will help to demystify other Africans for black South Africans. It showed people that all of us are very similar, even though we think we are different. We also need to encourage South Africans to visit other African countries."

He pointed out that many South African children, once they completed school, wanted to go only to Western countries such as Australia, America and England. "That is a problem, because we need to make sure that these children also go to other African countries such as Zimbabwe."

Rhoda Kadalie

Rhoda Kadalie felt that xenophobia came about because of South Africa's isolation from the rest of the continent. "We are the one African country that never interacted with our neighbours. We didn't have an exposure to Zimbabwe, Namibia, Burundi, Nigeria, Ghana and so on. The ignorance about black African countries is quite shocking and that is because of our political past and our political history. Black South Africans never expect another black to be a foreigner, so they immediately start to speak in their mother tongue to other black people. This is mainly because of having been isolated from other black countries for so many years.

"Xenophobia also has to do with unemployment: when people have no resources, no access to housing, jobs, education and health care, they will discriminate against foreigners. We have black-on-black discrimination purely around access to resources.

"It is also about ignorance of other people. It is easy to blame crime on the Zimbabweans, Moroccans or Nigerians who are coming to our country. But the big irony is that white firms in this country now find it better to employ foreign blacks to their own blacks. They believe foreign blacks are more docile, because they come with a different work ethic, and they won't challenge you in terms of the Labour Relations Act.

"[When] you walk around in Cape Town, you see Ethiopians working as security guards. I sometimes go to the companies and ask them why they don't employ their own blacks. They will tell you things like local blacks are too cocky, they want more money, the Labour Relations Act gives them too much power and at least the foreign blacks are happy to have a job. They are prepared to put up with exploitation, they are more reliable, more honest and they are not criminals.

"There is resentment among black South Africans that they are not employed. They ask the question: 'Why should others be employed when I could do the job?' But it is also about the skills that other black Africans bring into our country. We can't always assume that it is only white people who bring skills into this country. There are lots of black people who bring skills that we do not have. Otherwise these skilled people go overseas. I heard a frightening statistic that there are 300 000 African PhDs working abroad."

Carel Boshoff

"There is a reason for this huge influx of people into South Africa and there is a reason why poverty is a major problem. It is because resources are limited and scarce. And so there is competition for these resources.

"Politics exists because of borders. And borders, which restrict access to resources, create conflict. The simplistic but unrealistic solution would be to have no borders at all. But this would not solve the problem for those competing for access to the economy.

"I realise that there are also arguments against what I have said. There are those that say that immigrants normally have a positive influence on the economy, because someone who has walked for 2 000 kilometres is normally a motivated person who possesses determination and other skills which would benefit the economy.

"This topic is not my area of expertise, however, so I cannot speak with authority. But I can say that I would be careful about tackling a very complex material and political problem with a simple moralism that says we should all be nice to each other."

Melanie Verwoerd

Melanie Verwoerd could not understand why there was xenophobia in South Africa. "Usually xenophobia in other countries stems from a fear of otherness or differentness. For instance, in Ireland there used to be only Catholic, English-speaking whites and suddenly they had to deal with people who looked different and acted differently.

"I thought that we had dealt with that in South Africa. But I presume that xenophobia has to do with socio-economic demands. That is why I am saying it is not difficult to deal with multi-culturalism when things are going well economically. It's far harder when there is a scarcity of resources. It has become an issue in South Africa precisely because of that. There are just not enough resources to go around."

I asked her why it had suddenly become a problem, when we have always had an influx of people coming into South Africa, for instance, from Eastern Europe. Why is it only a problem now that people are coming from Africa?

"Maybe it is because many of them are coming in at a level where there is greater competition for resources," she said. "Maybe it is easier to accommodate people in big companies. This does not seem to bother anyone. But when they come in at the level of the hawkers on the street, the scarcity issue becomes important. Maybe it is linked to that. It is probably a lot more complicated than this."

Sielie and Kenny Nolan
Sielie Nolan had heard in the community that foreigners brought diseases such as Aids into South Africa.

Kenny Nolan said that the Western Cape had its own form of xenophobia. "The talk in the community, before the election in 1994, was that African people had been bussed into the Western Cape to vote, because the people in the ANC believed that there were too few Africans in the Western Cape. However, after the elections, many of them stayed in the Western Cape. This led to animosity among coloured people."

"Coloured people like to make up stories. They hear something, and then add their own little bit. This is how these stories just grow and grow," said Sielie Nolan.

"I would like the Nigerians to go back to their country, so that there will be more jobs for our people," said Kenny.

Sielie disagreed. "We cannot treat people like that. They are our neighbours. We must try to help them, because if we are in a similar situation, they can help us. Most of these people from other African countries have stalls where they sell cigarettes and other stuff. They came here with little help, yet they have opened their own businesses and they are not relying on the government to support them. We could have done the same, but we did not. We should not blame them for taking the initiative."

Vincent Barnes

Vincent Barnes said he'd had first-hand experience of how white immigrants had benefited under apartheid. "When I was working as an apprentice to become an artisan, we had an English foreman who had no idea what to do in the job. He had been living quite comfortably in South Africa for more than 20 years.

"In the old days, no one had problems with Europeans coming into the country, and it was just accepted that Europeans or Americans could be chief executives of South African companies.

"Now suddenly we have a problem when black Africans are coming into our country. This is only a problem for some people. For many years, we have had other nationalities coming into our country and it was never a problem. It should not be a problem now."

Leo de Souza and Obed Zilwa

"If you see a white tourist walking around, no one is going to say that he is here to take someone's job," said Leo. "If a white person from a country like Germany gets employed by a bank, for instance, no one is going to say that he is taking someone's job. It is only a problem when it comes to dark-skinned people.

"To a large degree, xenophobia can be blamed on poverty and unemployment. People see these Nigerians coming to South Africa, forgetting that these countries looked after our brothers when they were in exile. They forget this because they don't have any jobs. They are unemployed."

Obed saw many reasons for South Africans being xenophobic. "Nigerians and Moroccans have a reputation for being involved in criminal activities. They come into our countries and marry our sisters. Once they are married, they dump them and go fetch their wives. All they want is citizenship. These young girls fall pregnant and get treated very badly. In Johannesburg, in Hillbrow, it is even worse, with many people getting into drugs. They even start their own night clubs. If you go to these clubs, you are an outcast in your own country if you are not from Nigeria. Only South African girls are allowed.

"This is what happens, but not all Nigerians are bad people. Just because one Nigerian is a bad person, does not mean that the entire country of Nigeria is the same."

Leo added: "I think our criminal justice system is so screwed up that we are not dealing with the issue of crime properly. If there is a known criminal element and they are not being dealt with properly, perceptions are created and people get classified. What Obed was talking about was a Moroccan gang that was terrorising Sea Point, so the perception was created that all Moroccans are criminals."

"Ultimately, it is economic," she concluded.

Tracy-Lee Rosslind

"The first country that comes to mind when people talk about illegal aliens is Nigeria. Even at school, everybody talks about how the Nigerians are taking over Muizenberg and things like that.

"We already have a situation where we think the blacks are taking the jobs, the whites are taking the jobs, or the coloureds are taking the jobs. Now we are faced with the situation where people from a different country are coming in and are also posing a threat to jobs. It is basically job security that is at stake.

"Of course, people also have the perception that people who are coming from another country are drug dealers and criminals and that they are the ones who rape our children.

"I think our best response would be to take a firm stand in our immigration laws, to make sure that our borders are strict and that there is no corruption. It really is not impossible.

"However, one should not forget that South Africans, particularly the ANC, had a lot of allies in Africa in the past."

Keathelia Satto

Keathelia Satto had heard people saying that immigrants from other African countries carried Aids and other diseases.

"This is why people say they are opposed to these people coming into our country. But I don't believe that Africans carry diseases or have any special sickness. White people can also be the carriers of diseases."

My thoughts

Many African immigrants whose qualifications are not recognised in South Africa have been forced to resort to entrepreneurial means to survive. And in some cases, they have done much more than survive: they have actually created jobs for others.

An African immigrant who works as a car guard in Kalk Bay told me that he has two engineering degrees and speaks several languages, yet he has been unable to secure work in South Africa. He is thus forced to work as a car guard to put food on his family's table.

Discussions with foreign Africans who run stalls in the Cape Town city centre reveal the same thing: these are mainly highly-qualified individuals who cannot find work in the country they have chosen as their new home. Which makes one think: why, in a country such as South Africa, where there is a serious skills shortage in so many areas, can highly-qualified people not find work? Among these people are doctors, lawyers and engineers.

Surely our government should be encouraging people with skills to come and settle in our country? Surely we should be trying to make sure that people are welcome in our country? Surely we should be trying to harness the skills that these people offer to advance our country's development?

Yes, there is a shortage of resources in South Africa, but if we used these foreign skills properly, more resources could be generated and shared among more people.

The media also have a role to play in countering the xenophobia that exists in our country. The media need to do more than just report on instances of xenophobia; they need to educate people about the positive outcomes that could result from welcoming African immigrants into our country.

There is an assumption among the majority of South Africans, even those who consider themselves progressive, that all black immigrants are poor whereas whites from other countries are able to contribute to job creation and to the upliftment of the economy. Until we change this mindset, I believe xenophobia will remain a problem in South Africa.

CHAPTER 7
CAN RACISM EVER BE ELIMINATED?

Dealing with intolerance

How can one eliminate racism, and can it ever be done away with? I believe South Africa stands a chance of overcoming racism for the following reasons.

South Africa has one of the world's most progressive constitutions, which outlaws racial discrimination. It also has a vibrant civil society that helps to keep contentious issues in the public spotlight, and a range of parastatal organisations to deal with issues of racial, gender and other discrimination. These organisations include the Human Rights Commission and the Gender Commission. In addition, South Africa's government came to power on the basis of their opposition to apartheid and racial discrimination, and thus the issue of racism is on its agenda.

There also appears to be a realisation among many companies that we need to deal with our past, which means that we need to find ways of creating greater interaction and tolerance among all the people of our country. Companies dealing in diversity training have found that their services are much in demand.

The initiative that I launched at the *Cape Times* in 1998, called One City Many Cultures, was aimed at creating greater tolerance and understanding among the people of Cape Town. Since then, there have been several similar initiatives. Unfortunately, One City Many Cultures came to an end after I left the *Cape Times*. I believe that there is an ongoing need for similar projects if this country is to succeed in overcoming racism.

I asked my interviewees what they thought could be done to reduce racism and whether they thought it could ever be completely eliminated. I also asked them whether they believed there should be government intervention on the issue of racism or if it should be addressed by civil society.

Leo de Souza and Obed Zilwa

Leo de Souza believed that as long as our identities were hinged on skin colour or cultural groupings, there would be racism. "I don't think you are going to eliminate it for a very long time. The best thing we did was to make it illegal. It was a brilliant move, because it makes people conscious of it. We have to be in your face about racism. We must stop saying that maybe a racist person does not understand people and he must be given time. People have been given enough time."

Obed Zilwa added: "Not many people know that you cannot be called a "Kaffir", that you cannot be called a "coolie", that you cannot be called anything that you regard as racist.

"I believe that we must try to understand people," he continued. "This helps to get rid of racism." He mentioned, as an example, a *Cape Argus* photographer, an Afrikaner, who used to roll down his car window every time he saw Obed in the street and shout: "Hey, *kaffertjie*."

"I used to shout back at him and called him *rooinek*. Before he left the *Argus*, he went to management and begged them to give me his job. This is an Afrikaner who called me a Kaffir, and I got the job. He died soon after leaving the paper. A few hours before he closed his eyes, he called me and I was standing with him next to his bed.

"We understood each other; we got to know each other better. That is very important. Don't just judge a person by his colour. I have been to Afrikaans farms, those places where people speak only Afrikaans and they always look at blacks with suspicion. But the moment I speak to them, they change and they have a different perspective about me. Not about blacks, but about me. Imagine if more people could do that. Black people must not sit in the corner because they fear being called Kaffirs or Hotnots. We must get out there and challenge those who call us these names."

Leo suggested that racism should be addressed on all levels. "It should be a personal responsibility, a social responsibility, a political responsibility and a government responsibility. It is wonderful that the government has put laws in place, but I don't think there should be racist police. I think it is everybody's responsibility."

Obed felt that it was very important not to forget the workplace. "It is not something that is widely discussed. Let's take Newspaper House [the home of the *Cape Times* and *Cape Argus* newspapers] as an example. They had these workshops where we talked about racism and I said, 'Does the fact that my boss is a white man and he gives a certain job to a coloured photographer mean that he is giving that job to that photographer because he is coloured? And when they send me to Gugulethu, is it because I am black and know Gugulethu or is it because I am the first available photographer?'

"It is so important to deal with racism in the workplace, because you see those people eight hours every day except weekends. These are the people you would first look at as racist. Black people do this all the time. When they are told to do something or when they are told they are wrong, they immediately accuse you of racism."

Leo suggested that the dictum "each one teach one" should apply to dealing with racism: "I am a manager and I have all kinds of different races working under me. I had a serious problem between a Xhosa man and an Indian man. I actually identified what the problem was and it was language. They both spoke English, but the Indian man called the Xhosa man 'my friend' and he was very curt, so the Xhosa man thought the Indian man was disrespectful. I spoke to them and told them that I thought there was a cultural problem. This is the only way to do it."

Naledi Pandor

"I define racism as the ability of others to impact on my functioning in society. It is their ability to prevent me from acting in a particular way because of my colour. Given that, I believe that we can eliminate racism, but it means that we have to change our curriculum; it means we have to educate our society with the principles of what should become alive in our lives. This cannot be something that Mbeki or anyone else articulates. It must be something that each one of us strives towards. We have to start in schools, in our workplaces and in a range of domains.

"Government should pronounce itself very clearly and should show a commitment to non-racialism through policies and also in the way we conduct ourselves. When people visit our institutions, they should feel welcome.

"I have not been to Home Affairs recently, but I used to go there on a regular basis just to observe what was happening. I remember that they would have nobody to assist Xhosa-speaking people. The forms would all be in English. How did they expect a Xhosa-speaking person to fill them out? If we were really non-racial and diverse in our approach, we would also have a Xhosa-speaking staff member who was ready and available to assist an illiterate Xhosa person to complete those forms. I think there are steps that government can take."

Trevor Oosterwyk

"We have to create a society that is as equitable as possible. There must be potential and opportunities for all the people in South Africa, not just in the law but also in practice. It must be seen to be happening. Schools must be open, communities must be open. We have a lot to work out, but I believe it is possible and we are going to do it. I just think we have to deal with the distrust and ignorance of each other in our communities.

"If you look at the younger generation, Loyiso [the R&B star] is just as popular among coloured youth as African youth. Kaizer Chiefs is a popular team among both coloured and African youth, in the same way that Bafana Bafana, the Proteas cricket team and our national rugby team are supported by all races. Sport, culture and music provide the opportunity to eliminate racism.

"The more we can expose people to each other, to create that understanding of culture and of language, the more we are going to find that these prejudices will disappear. But in the same way, people need to be confident about themselves. They must be confident about who they are and not fear that what they had and what they are will be taken away. Then they will not have a need to be prejudiced and racist."

Trevor believed that government should provide the infrastructure, such as the judiciary and the police, to combat racism, but that ultimately it should be addressed by civil society. "Education is obviously an area where government can play a role, but I would rather see government making resources available to civil society so that people can do it for themselves.

"Government has to do with political parties, and political parties have vested interests. If, for instance, Ebrahim Rasool [the premier of the Western Cape] wants to do something, he wants people to vote for him and people will read it like that. Therefore I see that it is going to be far more powerful if the people who combat racism are not seen to want votes or are not working in the interest of any one political party or any particular government of the day. They should rather be working in the interest of people and that is why I support the notion of civil society."

Rhoda Kadalie

"I don't believe that racism can ever be eliminated," said Rhoda, "but a ruling party that has come from a system of racial domination can contribute enormously to dealing with the race issue."

"Mandela was very clever at race issues. Thabo Mbeki took over and took another turn. I think that's unfortunate because I think we need leadership on the racism issue. I once wrote an article about racism in conflict areas such as Burundi, Bosnia and Rwanda, and demonstrated that when you use race as a political tool, it gains a momentum of its own."

"That's why the United Nations Conference Against Racism was such a bad thing for the world and South Africa. There was no leadership: not from Nkosazana Zuma, not from Mbeki, nor from Mary Robinson. It generated more race hate than it mobilised against racism. Why? Because you must be honest about your own racism. You cannot point a finger at Israel and not do anything about Zimbabwe. You cannot talk about genocide in Israel when you are not prepared to stand up for the white farmers in Zimbabwe. What is bedevilling racial politics in this country are the double standards. That is why people rejected the Home for All campaign [a campaign to get white people to acknowledge that they benefited from apartheid], because the very people who pushed that campaign are in the President's pocket and they are silent about other atrocities."

Asked if there should be government intervention on racism, Rhoda pointed out that we already have state intervention. "This intervention is in the form of the Constitution, the Bill of Rights, the Human Rights Commission, the Gender Commission and the Public Protector. These are all mechanisms that we have. Where government intervenes, is to abide by its own rules.

"For instance, if there is a case in the public sector, you take it up and deal with it. That is the duty of government. The duty of government is to protect the vulnerable, the discriminated against and the elderly.

"Civil society, with the Bill of Rights, is meant to protect citizens against forms of discrimination. There is a vertical relationship between the State and citizens. There is also a relationship between citizen and citizen, and the citizens can also evoke those mechanisms.

"When the State intervenes it has to be very strategic in how it intervenes. But a government also has to lead by example. We cannot say we have a country based on democratic principles and then you have the African Nationalism of the kind that we have in South Africa. It is dangerous.

"You can't use the race card to excuse every other political misdemeanour. You are not allowed to diminish the historical struggle against racism by cheapening it in the way that we do. If you don't lead by example politically on the race question, then you have no right to intervene."

Wilmot James
"I think with greater knowledge and greater understanding, especially in the area of science, racism can be eliminated, because it is actually a meaningless construct that has come about as a result of colonialism and so on.

"This is really what one has to do. We don't believe the world is flat any more and the fact is that race is part of human variation determined by less than one per cent of our genetic material. We are 99 per cent the same, as a species, and our physical features are determined by less than one per cent of our overall genetic material. It's a meaningless biological category. There is no connection whatsoever to intelligence or ability. The problem is that people can't *see* it. But they can see that the earth is not flat.

Wilmot said that the way to deal with racism was through the law. "We have a series of legislation dealing with racism. We might want to have a discussion about whether the machinery is good enough. Is it good enough just to have these laws? Is the equity legislation good enough? If somebody is violated in a racial or another way, they can sue. The major problem here is that often people do not have the resources to take cases to court. Civil society can help in that instance. By law, the Human Rights Commission should be able to do that. I think we have adequate laws. It is just a matter of making sure that individuals have access to the courts.

"Of course, if you want to say the [court] machinery is not good enough, then that is a completely different discussion."

Phatekile Holomisa
Phatekile suggested that racism could be drastically reduced through education. "People who are educated don't have a problem, and don't have insecurities. Some people are racist because they are insecure and they feel threatened. They think that if another person prospers, they will be adversely affected in the sense that some of their possessions

may be taken away."

"If you are educated, it is different. Education gives you confidence in yourself and the ability to talk to anyone and to interact with anyone. If there is education and, of course, the equitable distribution of resources, that will go a long way towards reducing levels of racism."

As for government intervention, Phatekile thought it was necessary "only insofar as it addresses the core causes of racism, which are inequality and the unequal distribution of resources. Government should intervene through education, and providing as many opportunities as possible for everybody to be self-sufficient.

"Of course, if someone swears at another person, then government must intervene. Already there are laws against swearing at another person or against the assault of another person, regardless of what the cause is. At that level it is the responsibility of government, but it is for civil society to learn to respect; to inculcate respect for other human beings."

Carel Boshoff

Asked if racism could ever be eliminated, Carel said it depended on what was meant by the word "eliminate".

"If you are talking about a society where a few free-spirited individuals will associate with each other without any consciousness of distinguishing features or race, then I would say that is a fantasy which does not exist.

"I feel that the problem of racism could be dealt with if one recognised the various identities that people have at various times of their lives. These identities do not only relate to race. They also relate to economic status and cultural activities. I think if we can overcome the emphasis on a factor of identity distinction, then maybe we can begin to look at the relationship between the various distinguishing factors that exist between people. But I don't believe racism can ever be completely done away with."

Carel said his approach to the issue of government intervention on racism was "probably conservative". He explained, "I believe that government should establish a certain context of human rights, of laws that place everyone on the same footing. The cultural question, the political question and the moral question need to be left to civil society to address.

"I must add that I believe we would have the greatest success in addressing racism as a problem if we saw it as a political problem and not as a moral problem."

Melanie Verwoerd

"I don't think we should try to stifle racism, because then we will just push it under the carpet," said Melanie. "The most important thing is to be conscious of it. People need to be aware that we should not fear those who are different to us. We need to embrace our differences, but people don't do that instinctively. The topic of racism needs to stay in our education system and in our media."

Melanie reckoned that racism should be tackled by both government and civil society. "On the one hand, the government needs to monitor itself constantly, because it is our final safeguard. But in the end, dealing with racism is not something that government can do on its own. Too often, people sit back and wait on government to do something."

Kenny and Sielie Nolan

Sielie said it was clear that the black government had improved certain things in society and was already dealing with racism. "The black government has taken away apartheid and improved things. There were places that we, as coloureds, could not go to, such as white beaches. They have made it possible for us to go to these places," she said. "However, there are cases where I feel the black government has gone too far, for instance in legalising abortion and prostitution. I don't think that is right."

Kenny was convinced that the community should take responsibility in tackling racism. Sielie at first disagreed: "The government began everything by shifting our people and throwing everyone on a heap. So it plays a big role. It can help by improving things, because it started everything."

When it was pointed out to her that she was talking about the old government, she said: "The government can still help, but the community has to learn to live together. We have to take responsibility to sort out these problems."

Vincent Barnes

"I doubt very much whether racism can be eliminated. You will always have instances of racism," said Vincent.

"We can see it happening, even in Parliament, and it comes from both sides. I don't think it is going to go away. If one looks at a supposedly free country like England, or a country like Italy, and you see how they boo black players, call them monkeys and throw bananas on the field, then you realise that racism is not going to go away. It will always be there.

"However, I think the youth is going to make a big difference. That is where it is starting, because they have a chance and they are innocent. They are growing up accepting people who are different to them. Culture is changing and they are at the forefront of that change.

"When we used to play and someone would put on rap music, then there would always be someone shouting that we should put it off. Now you have white players also listening to rap music. The younger generation is growing up differently to the way we grew up. We must not try to enforce our ways on them."

Vincent said that government intervention on racism was crucial. "We are led by what we learn in the government schools. If we learn anything positive or negative, it has a serious effect on the public. Government has to be involved in the fight against racism. It needs to send the correct messages to all of us."

Athena and Manny Sotomi

Athena was of the opinion that racism would never be eliminated. "It is an age-old problem and it is not something new to South Africa or particularly unique to South Africa. Although it could be unique in terms of the depth to which it was practised here."

Manny said that racism was unique in South Africa because it had been legislated. "In the United States, it was implied in legislation, but in South Africa, it was formally legislated.

"If you look at the countries I have lived in, particularly the United States and Britain, then I believe South Africa has the best potential to deal with racism. In Britain, nothing has been done about racism and it has become increasingly sophisticated and underground because it is illegal. In America it is not as sophisticated, but America is a very legalistic country and you have legal recourse. If you call me 'nigger' and other people witness it, I will sue you for everything you have.

"In South Africa it is sometimes blatant, which is probably a good thing, because it allows us to deal with it. I hope we don't drive it underground, because then it will just become more sophisticated."

Manny and Athena agreed that there should be intervention from both government and civil society in addressing racism. "Legislation should be tested to set a benchmark to alert people – black, white or coloured – to know that when they go beyond a certain point they could end up spending years in jail," suggested Manny. "I think we need to impose jail sentences on people who are racist. If people are only fined, everyone can go around calling people 'Kaffir' and just pay the fine."

Khusta and Karen Jack

Khusta Jack postulated that education could be used in attempts to eradicate racism. "However, I believe the government has failed to integrate education and to use it to integrate South African society. For example, all the schools in the Eastern Cape have almost no black teachers teaching in white schools. Also, there are very few whites teaching in black schools," he said. "In Port Elizabeth, where black people make up about 80 or 84 per cent of the population, the black teachers are in white schools, if they are there, only to teach IsiXhosa and nothing else.

"The government has to embark on a conscious effort to distribute teachers correctly. You cannot have a situation where one section of the community is taught by only that section of the community, especially with the kind of baggage we have.

"This is one area where the government has failed dismally. How are these kids going to appreciate what South Africa is by learning from people who grew up in a South Africa that was limited, that was discriminating, that saw black people as inferior, that thought that the system was right, and who were brought up in that system? They will just perpetuate racism, unless this situation is radically remedied.

"The government has the responsibility to normalise things. They can intervene in areas such as education and affirmative action.

"The society we live in is a capitalist society and if all black people are poor and they are thieves, and they are seen to be thieves, you can forget about it – you will never be able to win them over. The only way to work this society is to re-engineer it, because it was engineered to be what it is today."

Karen believed that civil society had a huge role to play in combating racism. "They must express their outrage at racism. They should have the avenues to express themselves when something happens."

Tracy-Lee Rosslind

"Racism will never be eliminated," said Tracy-Lee. "We listen to our parents and they came from apartheid. They taught us about apartheid and we will teach our children and the circle will continue forever. I don't think racism will ever be eliminated, but it is time to start teaching people that it is okay to be who you are.

"This does not mean that we are now saying that we are all the same, because we are not all the same. That is the mistake that everybody is making. Not being racist does not mean that you have to think you are the exact same person as another person. I can have the same kind of skin as you and I can be completely different. You [as a black person] can have the same ideals as someone who comes from a white family. If there were three coloured children, one raised in a coloured family, one raised in a black family, and one raised in a white family, we would have the same skin but would all be totally different. It comes down to your cultural beliefs, your traditions, your whole family situation."

Tracy-Lee felt that racism should be addressed by civil society as well as government. "When we can respect our leaders, when we can accept that they are doing a good job and that they know what they are talking about, then things will come right. We need to educate the people about government, to show them that our government did not come out of Standard Three and then got positions because of the struggle. When people trust their government, things will start to improve.

"The provinces need to sort out their racism issues and then the [central] government can get involved and teach people about racism."

Keathelia Satto

Keathelia Satto felt that racism could be eliminated, but not completely. "People must come around to schools to lecture on racism. They come and lecture about all kinds of other stuff at school. Maybe they can put something on TV to show parents what to do, for instance, if their children got insulted because of their colour."

She believed that the government should intervene on the issue of racism. "They are the head of the country and should do something about it. The community should do something about it too, but with the government's help. They [the government] can help by providing money to help solve the problems related to racism."

My thoughts

I was speaking to American author Nathan McCall about the lessons we could learn from Americans about eliminating racism, and he laughed and said, "We have been dealing with this issue for decades and we still haven't got it right." In South Africa, of course, racism was legally abolished just over a decade ago. Whether it will ever be possible to eliminate racism from society completely, however, is another issue.

Shortly after South Africa became a democracy, some South Africans were reluctant to talk about race. This resulted, I believe, in us ignoring the problems of race and racism. Quite often, one would speak to South Africans, particularly white South Africans, who would say things like: "Why do you always talk about race? That belongs to the past. There is no need to bring up the past. We must look towards the future." Sometimes they would add: "Just look at Nelson Mandela.

He holds no grudges about how he was treated in the past. Why can't you be more like Nelson Mandela?"

The problem is that, unlike Nelson Mandela, the majority of South Africans are still suffering the effects of South Africa's racist past. These effects can be seen in the townships where black people still live in poverty. They can be seen on the street corners of the townships where hundreds of able-bodied young people lounge around because they are unable to find work.

Through proper communication and education, we could at least reduce racism, but this is not something that is going to happen overnight. It will require the joint effort of government, civil society and the entire South African population.

CHAPTER 8
LANGUAGE AND RACE

An important turning point: 1976

The year 1976 was an important turning point for many people. In June of that year, students in Soweto protested against, among other things, the imposition of Afrikaans as a language of instruction in their schools. The protests spread throughout the country and eventually led to the apartheid government dropping their plans to impose Afrikaans on the people of Soweto, most of whom did not want to be taught in Afrikaans, even if they spoke the language at home.

Up until 1976, I had spoken mainly Afrikaans, but I took a decision that year to stop speaking the language, which I identified as the language of the oppressor. I was still forced to speak Afrikaans in school, because it was, along with English, promoted as an official language. But outside of school, I tried to ignore the language completely.

Recently, however, I have learnt that Afrikaans is, in fact, a language that originated among the coloured community of the Western Cape. Slowly, I have begun to speak Afrikaans more actively again.

I have also learnt that many Africans actually speak a dialect of Afrikaans known as *tsotsitaal*. I have often sat in on conversations in Johannesburg where African people were speaking in Sotho or Xhosa, and been able to follow the conversation because of the many Afrikaans and English words they used. Sometimes I would surprise them by making a contribution when they all thought that I would not be able to understand what they were talking about.

One of the things that I have noticed in my travels overseas is that whenever I bump into expatriate South Africans, they immediately speak Afrikaans to me. In some ways, speaking Afrikaans abroad makes one feel more at home.

One of the first things the ANC government did when it came into power was to declare that there were eleven official languages in South Africa. These eleven languages include English, Afrikaans, Xhosa, Zulu, Sotho and a host of other indigenous languages spoken mainly in particular provinces. While giving all these languages official status was meant to protect them, in reality, English has become the "unofficial official" language of South Africa, and the other languages are struggling to survive.

The development of English as South Africa's official language should go hand in hand with the notion of developing a South African culture that would include elements from all or most of the cultures that exist in South Africa today.

I asked my interviewees whether, in a situation where English has effectively become the lingua franca of South Africa, the other languages will be able to survive. Is it possible to protect the other languages, and should they be protected?

Khusta and Karen Jack

"There are many untested theories floating around about language in South Africa," said Khusta Jack. "For example, there is a belief that you cannot be anybody unless you speak English, and that has really been enforced into the minds of many South Africans.

"When I address public meetings, I intentionally speak in IsiXhosa, especially if there are Xhosa-speaking people in the audience or if the minority of the people present is English-speaking. The reason for this is that I have seen how confident and how happy one can be with your speech if you say things in your own language rather than battling in a second or third language.

"If a language is not yours, it will never be yours. No matter how much you try to perfect it, you will find it difficult to be as comfortable as you can be in your mother tongue.

"When you throw your language away, you throw away many things, such as your culture, your stories and your identity. Everything goes with it.

"You can pick up the wealth of a language from the songs that people sing. For instance, when the British team plays and they are winning, you can hear the English singing *Rule Britannia*.

"When we sing *Shosholoza*, we tell a story about what happened to us as we were crossing the fields and mountains on the way to the gold mines. These are the kinds of things that would be lost if you killed a language. You would kill the history of a people."

Karen Jack said that at her son's school, one of the problems was that the children whose home language was Xhosa were learning Xhosa at the same pace as the English-speaking white children. "They have lost their Xhosa completely. However, on the other hand, languages are always on the move, and maybe in 300 years time South Africa will have one language with lots of elements of all the languages. I think, to a certain extent, it is something you cannot actually control."

Khusta said he accepted Karen's view, but that the disturbing thing for him was that people were saying you could not be successful unless you spoke English. "That is not true. There are smaller nations in Europe with five million people, or even two million people that don't speak English, yet they are big nations in every respect. The German Chancellor will not battle with English, which he can speak, because he wants to be comfortable speaking his own language.

"The people from the Arab countries speak their own languages. Here, because of the cultural enslavement and domination of our minds, we believe that we have to speak English, otherwise we cannot do business.

"When the English came to do business here, they couldn't speak a word of IsiXhosa and many of them still can't, even to this day. They just forced everyone to learn their language."

Karen said that her home language was English, which is what she spoke to her children. "They are not bilingual, but they do speak

Xhosa as a second language. We found with friends that if the mother is Xhosa and the father is English, the children will be bilingual. But in our home, Xhosa will be a strong second language and that's the way it is. Also, Khusta forgets to speak Xhosa to the kids."

I told them about my eight-year-old daughter who, when I asked her whether she was doing better in Afrikaans or Xhosa, replied "Xhosa". That, for me, was also a sign that things were changing in our country. Khusta agreed and said that he believed Afrikaans was going to suffer because of the policy of having eleven official languages. "Many people believe that speaking Afrikaans is speaking the language of the oppressor," he said.

Khusta recounted a story of how he once spoke Afrikaans to a five-year-old boy. "We were at a children's event and he insisted on speaking Afrikaans to me. His father kept on telling him to speak English to me, but he refused. I can speak Afrikaans quite well and I continued to speak to the boy in Afrikaans. Even his brothers and sisters were speaking Afrikaans. It was clear that they were an Afrikaans family. I did not understand why his father was telling him to speak English to me."

"Maybe he was embarrassed," said Karen. Khusta agreed. "Yes, maybe he was embarrassed to speak Afrikaans in public."

Trevor Oosterwyk

"At a superficial level, as a daily discourse, it is true that English can play this unifying role, but to develop proficiency in that language is a problem.

"What percentage of Capetonians, other than white people, is really proficient in that language? Even the coloured middle class do not have a great proficiency in the language. Maybe we don't need a high level of proficiency; maybe we just need a working knowledge and the ability to use the language.

"The pedagogues and the educationists, however, will tell you that if a language is not spoken in the house where the child grows up, it is not useful to send this child to a school in that language. That becomes a problem, because you are never going to develop people who are capable of having a strong command over any of the languages.   ·

"I think the long-term objective is for us to develop English as the lingua franca. But whether that is the objective or not, society is just doing it. That is the problem with having the policy of eleven official languages. The government just does not have the money to really give meaning to it. So English is just going to colonise it, if you will, or take over and assert itself. It will happen.

"I wrote a piece on the mother-tongue task team which aims to implement mother-tongue education at schools. However, the problem is that most people send their children to English-medium schools. Xhosa and Afrikaans are not seen as useful languages to learn. You can look at the newspapers, the magazines, the notices in the cities and in the businesses. The payoff is just not there, and if it is not there, people are not going to buy in.

"People must see themselves reflected in society. We need to make the city more non-racial."

Phatekile Holomisa

Phatekile Holomisa was not sure whether language had been used as a tool to further entrench racism in our country. "I know the Afrikaners tried to foist Afrikaans on us as a medium of instruction, but that was a once-off thing. It was aborted because the students revolted against it. The problem is that our languages have not been developed by the authorities in the past to be on the same level as English. That is a tricky matter, even for a non-racial government," he said.

"We talk of the need to promote the languages, but who will speak those languages except the people who already speak them? We need to communicate with people who belong to other language groups.

"If we are told to promote the eleven languages, we will promote them where we are. AmaXhosa will promote Xhosa and understand it among themselves, as will the AmaZulu, AmaSotho and AmaVenda. It is good for the members of those language groups to understand their language and to speak it and hear it, but it does not assist in communicating with others or in developing languages.

"In my view, English is unfortunately going to become the language that is common among all of us. There would be a problem if it was decided that one of the African languages should be promoted. Then the question would be, which language? The Zulus might say, 'We are the largest single language group,' but the others would say, 'No, it cannot be. Just because we are a minority does not mean that our culture is inferior to any other.'

"Perhaps if we have at least three languages in a province, that might work. In the Western Cape for instance, because of the predominance of Xhosa among black Africans and the predominance of Afrikaans among the coloureds and some whites, we could teach Xhosa, Afrikaans and English. The same would be the case in the Eastern Cape. In KwaZulu-Natal we could have Zulu, English and Afrikaans. English has to be one of the languages."

Carel Boshoff

Carel Boshoff agreed that English was becoming the lingua franca in South Africa. He explained that this had implications for the definition of Afrikaners.

"What I mean is that those in power have defined themselves and they have tried to force their definition of themselves on everybody else. I get the impression that English as the lingua franca, and the common culture that could be developing in South Africa, will basically be the language and the culture of a limited elite.

"That the state will in future play more of a role in determining language and culture assumes the typical national state idea, as it appeared in the European context, and where it brutally oppressed minorities and minority cultures.

"On the one hand I hope that that does not happen because that kind of oppression will only lead to a whole lot of resistance. Whether it is successful or not, it will lead to a tremendous loss of language and collective heritage, with many common group stories and wisdoms being lost along with the languages. It will just make our universe so much smaller. On the other hand, I don't know if it can still happen. I don't know if the South African state has the ability to do this.

"Maybe what will happen is that in the metropolitan areas, the cultural ideas of the elite will dominate, while in the rural areas, people will just continue as in the past in their own vernacular languages and keep their own cultures and cultural institutions intact. I don't think we are going to become like France where they had a very successful and centralised destruction of minorities.

"In South Africa we have to subject the centralised national state to a reasonably thorough critique. We need to find a system that takes into account the reasonable limitations that states have today. This translates into practical, executable, underlying relations between languages and cultures. We should then be able to produce a certain common image and that image cannot do anything other than represent the diversity that is part the image of the rainbow nation, as some people have called it."

Rhoda Kadalie

"Languages will survive if there is a role for them. I don't believe in this policy of eleven official languages. Nowhere in the world do you have this. It's madness. What romanticising this notion really does is give black people false hope once again. We must accept that English is the global language of communication, whether we love it or hate it.

"We have a country where one per cent of the chartered accountants are black. What percentage of doctors is black? If you want to compete globally and internationally, we have to get our children to master English. We have to make English compulsory and make another language compulsory. We don't need Afrikaans, but Afrikaans will survive. You must give people a choice around Afrikaans and the other languages.

"We are not going to get anything right by insisting that we have eleven official languages. We must make Zulu and Xhosa our two strong indigenous languages. The others can exist and they will survive if they have to. But I don't think that a country needs to make a lot of effort to make languages survive if they are struggling.

"If you look at Xhosa, it isn't a very strong scientific language. We can say we are going to develop it, we can make a positive effort to upgrade the language, but then we must put our money where our mouths are.

"We can't just say we are going to have eleven official languages and then put nothing into it. If we are going to make them official, then we have to contend with the exigencies of the international global market."

Wilmot James

Wilmot James grew up in the rural areas of the Western Cape and spoke Afrikaans as a child. He found that this was a problem when he came to Cape Town, not because he spoke Afrikaans, but because of the brand of Afrikaans that he spoke. "I spoke Afrikaans with a Paarl accent," he explained. "In Standard Three I wanted to switch in the middle of the year from Afrikaans to English. My parents were teachers and they always spoke English at home, so the switchover from Afrikaans to English was actually quite easy for me.

"I have always thought of Afrikaans as my *taal* [language]. I am sorry I don't speak it as often as I should, but when I was at the *Cape Argus*, I would often go into the smoking room and find myself easing very comfortably into it. We would talk with an idiom that other people could understand. I think coloured people are mostly tolerant of cultural diversity."

I asked him whether he felt that people who had rejected Afrikaans, for instance in 1976, were now more comfortable with speaking the language.

"People are a lot more relaxed. The ability to communicate is probably one of the defining features of being a human, so you want to feel comfortable in the language that you speak. You learn your languages when you are young, and if you learnt to speak Afrikaans as a first language when you were young, typically that would be your comfort zone.

"The problem is that the Afrikaners politicised the whole thing and messed it all up. For them to now want to define us as brown Afrikaners is not on. I would tell them to go to hell.

"I don't think of myself as an Afrikaner, but I am Afrikaans speaking. I would have lost that language but because you learn it so young you never lose it. Language belongs to the people who speak it."

Melanie Verwoerd

Melanie Verwoerd, an Afrikaner by birth, said she spoke English for the sake of inclusiveness. "This is why you are writing your book in English, because you know that it would only sell so much or be read by so many if you wrote it in Afrikaans or any other African language," she told me.

"I always make an effort to speak Afrikaans because it is part of my identity. I guess I should be learning how to speak other African languages, because that would send a message, but I have not.

"I get quite annoyed and irritated if somebody tells me that Afrikaans should not have a place in our society. It should have a place, but its place should not be privileged. It is fine to speak Afrikaans as long as it is not used to exclude people. This is why I objected to the concept of a white Afrikaans university, which would just become a conservative white university.

"The other thing about language is that people have to keep it alive. It is not up to the government to keep languages alive. They need to put things in place to assist languages, such as laws to protect them, but then it is up to the people to keep them alive.

"We need to teach our children the language, the writers need to write in the language, the actors need to act in the language, and the playwrights need to write plays in the language. If it is worthwhile, it will continue.

"But Afrikaners should be careful of antagonising the mainstream of society by being oversensitive about Afrikaans. It is different if we say that this language is just something that we want to speak and that we want our children to speak."

Tracy-Lee Rosslind

"If you go to any other country in the world and cannot speak their language, you are bound to find people who can speak English, because it is a universal language. But like other countries in the world, we need to preserve our own languages. Afrikaans was enforced on our people, and I normally get my shield up when people speak about Afrikaans, but it must be protected. We need to protect our black languages as well. We learn Xhosa in school, but I think there should be more South African languages offered.

"I think it is ridiculous that Afrikaans should be considered as a second language. We established that English is an important language, because it is used throughout the world. Afrikaans is only used here, in the same way as other languages such as Xhosa and Zulu are only used here. Why should one of those languages not become our second language?

"We should be teaching children to speak Xhosa from a younger age. I started learning Xhosa in Sub A [Grade One] and I still cannot speak Xhosa, but I can speak Afrikaans. This is because the schools do not teach it properly. They do not teach it in a way that you can hold a proper conversation with somebody. They teach Xhosa like a textbook language. We should be doing more orals and we should be having more interaction with Xhosa-speaking people. We should not just learn about sentence structure and where your verb and predicate go. Xhosa is a language that needs to be spoken, and we need to learn how to speak it properly. Xhosa needs to be given the same respect and the same status because it is spoken in the same way as Afrikaans."

Keathelia Satto
Keathelia felt that South Africans should learn to speak English, while they could still speak other languages at home. "We do not need all these languages. I know that maybe if we were all able to speak Xhosa, it could help us to get a better understanding of people, but some of these languages are also difficult to learn. Sometimes in Xhosa they take an English or Afrikaans word and just twist it a little. So why can't everything just be in English or Afrikaans?

"English is an easy language to learn. Some of the Xhosa children at our school don't even write in Xhosa because it is such a difficult language. They prefer to write in English.

"People can continue to speak their own languages in their homes, but when they communicate with other people, they should rather speak English."

Athena and Manny Sotomi

Manny and Athena believed that language development, and especially the protection of smaller languages, had to start at home.

However, Athena suggested that others could contribute. "For instance, book publishers can assist by publishing books in indigenous languages." Manny pointed out that it would be difficult to promote books in indigenous languages. "Ultimately, it boils down to whether people will be prepared to buy books in indigenous languages."

Manny felt that while the government spoke about promoting eleven official languages, they did not make this a priority.

My thoughts

One of the ways in which the apartheid government made people like me feel estranged from the majority of the people in this country was by using language against us: by educating us in different languages so that we could not understand each other.

It was, of course, by design of our former rulers that I could not speak Xhosa. In fact, in the community where I grew up, it was not considered "cool" to even attempt to speak Xhosa, even though our inability to speak this language made it difficult for us to interact with a large section of the population. We were kept apart by more than freeways and railway lines. We were kept apart by our inability to speak each other's languages.

There are some people who will argue that it has been many years since I came to this realisation and that, in the meantime, I could have done something about it: I could have learnt how to speak Xhosa. Those who understand languages will know that it is very difficult to learn a new language as an adult. I tried to learn Zulu when I lived in KwaZulu-Natal, and it was one of the most difficult things I have had to do.

There are, of course, others who believe that languages such as Xhosa are overrated and should be treated simply as regional languages. Why, they ask, do we give so much attention to Xhosa when it is clear that English is the lingua franca of our country? One reason is the fact that

English is an international language. But the debate around language, especially in a complex society such as South Africa, is never an easy one. One cannot just allow languages to die out, because when they die, parts of their accompanying culture and tradition die with them.

Yet how much attention must the government give to different languages, especially the smaller ones? And what sort of role should civil society play in the protection of languages? This is probably a subject that needs a book of its own.

CHAPTER 9
RACISM IN THE MEDIA

'We were all in the struggle ...'

When the South African Human Rights Commission (SAHRC) held their hearings on racism in the media in 2000, I was vice-chairperson of the South African National Editors' Forum (Sanef), the organisation representing most South African editors. I was also the person leading Sanef's negotiations with the SAHRC at a time when there were all kinds of tensions in the media industry around the proposed hearings.

Most white editors were opposed to the hearings, while most black editors were in favour of them. The white editors were in the majority at the time and, to force them to testify at the hearings, the SAHRC considered issuing subpoenas against them. It was left to me and a few others within Sanef to negotiate with the SAHRC and to convince them that it was a bad idea to issue subpoenas against editors.

Finally, the SAHRC agreed not to pursue the subpoenas if the editors testified willingly, and the hearings were able to continue.

What happened at the hearings, however, convinced me that we still have a long way to go in terms of transforming the media industry and ridding it of racism and racist elements. White editor after white editor talked about how there was no racism at their publications and how they had all contributed to the struggle against apartheid.

As I listened to their presentations, I thought about how I had had to start my career at a paper focusing on the coloured community, because I could not get a job at the *Cape Argus* or the *Cape Times*, which were both papers aimed at white people. Both papers seemed to have a quota of black staff, which was never more than two or three, and when I started as a journalist, that quota was already filled. This irony was lost on most people when I eventually became editor of the *Cape Times*.

I thought about how most newsrooms, even at the most liberal of newspapers, the *Rand Daily Mail*, had been segregated and how the staff had had to use separate canteens. I thought about the stories told to me by Godfrey Heynes, one of the stalwarts of the *Cape Times*. Godfrey, now retired, was the first black sub-editor and later the first and only black chief sub-editor at the *Cape Times*. He told me about how he'd had to use a separate toilet in the works department because the toilet on the editorial floor was reserved for whites only.

I thought about the story Moegsien Williams (editor of *The Star*, a Johannesburg-based daily newspaper) had told me about a white woman who worked with him at the *Cape Argus*. She would always speak to him at the tea trolley, but when she saw him outside in the street, she would look away and pretend not to see him.

I thought about the fact that most of the major newspapers in South Africa were more than 100 years old and that, for most of those 100-odd years, they had excluded the majority of the population. Only recently had they made tentative, and not necessarily genuine, moves to include the black majority.

I thought about the newsroom and the top structure that I inherited when I became editor of the *Cape Times* and how overwhelmingly white it was. And I thought about the resistance from the white staff when I employed the first Africans at the *Cape Times*. The story went around that I wanted to replace all the white staff with blacks. I had to call a meeting where I told the staff that I had no intention of replacing competent white people with incompetent black people. However, I said, I would replace incompetent white people with competent black people. I said that I could not edit a paper where the staff demography did not match the demography of the population.

I thought about all of this as I listened to the white editors talk about how racism did not exist in their newspapers. I realised then that the struggle against racism in the media was a long, hard struggle that was probably only just beginning.

The SAHRC, of course, found that there *was* racism in the media, and made a whole range of recommendations, most of which have been ignored by the media bosses and editors. Part of the reason for this could possibly be blamed on the SAHRC itself, for the clumsy manner in which they put the hearings together. But I believe that most of the blame lies with the media practitioners who refuse to admit that racism in the media exists.

Racism can be found in its content, which actively ignores black people unless they do something wrong. It can also be found in the staffing of most of the publications. For instance, most of the sub-editors at South African publications are white and hold immense power over what is finally published.

The new racism in South Africa is also evident where media houses actively pursue African candidates for editorships, often overlooking better candidates, which sometimes leads to disastrous results. For instance, one African editor had to resign when it was discovered that he was a partner in a public relations firm on the side.

I believe that racism in the media will only be eradicated if there is commitment from editors and media owners to do something about it. They have to implement internal monitoring mechanisms. However, I do not have much confidence in the media's ability to monitor themselves, partly because editors nowadays have much broader responsibilities. Most editors are effectively business managers or managing directors of their newspapers, having to worry about staffing, advertising and circulation. They are thus unable to prioritise dealing with racism in the media.

I asked my interviewees whether there was racism in the media and, if so, how it manifested itself. I also asked them what could be done to counteract it.

Wilmot James

"I don't believe that racism in the media is intentional. A lot of it happens by default. One area of discussion is to look at staffing profiles: Who is being hired, who is being dismissed and what different strategies are being used within different media companies? One can also look at the top structure in the media, for instance the editors, deputy editors and associate editors, and look at their profiles.

"One has to ask the question: Why is there not enough investment in black people with talent and women with talent to make it possible to have more black people in the media?

"Then there is also the selection of news items and how one pursues news items. I don't know if it is racism, but it is certainly a problem that our lives, as we experience them across the spectrum, are not always reflected in the newspapers. There is a skewed representation given."

Asked what could be done to counteract racism in the media, Wilmot responded: "It will be much better if there is greater local ownership over certain parts of the media, but that is only part of the answer.

"The other part of the answer is really an appeal, an urging or an injunction, to the media industry to invest in people with talent and to deliberately seek out black people, and especially black women, for our newsrooms."

Trevor Oosterwyk

"The first problem is in the ownership of the media. If people other than whites do not own the media, then this is a big problem, and it is a problem of racism. If people's stories, black stories, are not told in the media, then this is all about excluding people, which amounts to racism. If we have more black people who own media, you will have a different group of people who think differently about who they employ, who they make managers and what to do at different levels.

"Interestingly, the number of stories in the *Cape Argus* that come from Khayelitsha and Gugulethu has increased greatly in the past few months, partly because we now have journalists who come from those areas. That shows you that the exclusion can come to an end when you start employing people from those areas.

"That's their world and they will reflect their world. We will now begin to get a diversity of stories, not even opinions and voices, just stories about things that happen in these communities. This means that our media can then become reflective of society in terms of its demographics.

"Now the problem is not so much that you don't have black people on your staff any more. The problem is the hierarchy. In most cases, the black journalists are your junior journalists and their ability to influence the newspaper is next to nothing. When your top structure is white and they are still working in the interest of the white community, that's a problem. I am very worried about the sub-editors at newspapers. They are ultimately the filters putting together the end product, and the creators of the final product. Yet they are not neutral filters. They can twist and turn facts and influence the product. Yet there are not enough black people in the subs' rooms. There are mainly whites. All those things need to be looked at."

Trevor said the question of foreign ownership and globalisation was a difficult one. "I believe that globalisation is inevitable and all globalisation is not necessarily bad. But it seems to me that if the media are owned by foreign companies, the way Independent Newspapers is at the moment, South Africans cannot mould it [the media] and take it in the direction that they want."

I asked him what could be done about racism in the media. "Transformation in the media is focused a lot on fast-tracking the employment of black journalists. Our problem is not that we cannot recruit, but that we are not creating the space for black journalists to express themselves. They remain junior reporters with no real influence on the newspapers.

"That's one area that should be dealt with. Increasingly, we need to begin to tell the stories of our communities in a way that has never been done before. I like what has happened in the electronic media. The South African soapies have begun to portray black people differently. Suddenly black people live in big houses, they wear fancy clothes and are the managing directors of corporates. That affects people's conceptions of who black people are. One of these soapies, *Generations*, is so popular in the coloured community, yet it is about the trials, tribulations and love affairs of black people. People identify with them and in this way we can start dealing with our perceptions of who we are.

"We need to start celebrating black achievement, even if it means that we must redefine what is newsworthy. But there must be an attempt to begin to give a different meaning to what "black" means in this society. Does black always mean the rapist, does it always mean the criminal, and does it always mean the poor guy who stands on the corner, or the street kid? This is what most of our stories about black people are about.

"We need a greater variety of black voices, not only African voices. We need more black voices that will also be critical of government. The problem is that those who are critical of government are mainly white."

Khusta and Karen Jack

Karen Jack said she could only speak about the media in the Eastern Cape. "The people who are employed are of the old order. They want to protect their status and don't see the good in anything that an ANC government will do. The amazing thing is that they don't see themselves as racist.

"There is also racism in the things that they leave out. You still have white babies on the front page, but if there is a major event like a jazz festival in the township, it will not make the paper. The newspapers focus only on the white community and only white people's views are expressed in the paper.

"Khusta writes in the paper and he gets lambasted, even personally, because his views are so alien to the community.

"I think racism in the media can be easily reversed and addressed. It is just a matter of will. But I know that if you sell newspapers, if your circulation numbers are going up, then nothing will be done about it."

Khusta believed that things would change with the economic

advancement of people who had been left out of the economy in the past. "The argument is that white people have disposable income at the moment. The sponsors happen to be white businessmen, and all these guys come from white, private schools. You don't have marketing directors and people like that coming from Bishop Lavis, Umlazi or Langa.

Karen interjected: "What about Johnnic? They are black and they own the Eastern Cape papers."

Khusta responded: "No, Johnnic is a black empowerment deal. The black owners at Johnnic are just frontmen. They have no impact on the editorial. They have put no money into the business, so they have no say. They have no money. It is just token ownership, really.

"These big so-called empowerment deals like Nails (New Africa Investment Limited) and Rails (Real Africa Investment Limited) are nothing more than shock absorbers to protect white capital. Until that picture is changed in real terms, and not in nominal terms, we are going to have a problem."

Leo de Souza and Obed Zilwa

Leo de Souza and Obed Zilwa disagreed completely on the issue of racism in the media.

"How can you say there is no racism in the media?" Leo asked Obed. "You know it is driven by economic policies. It is about what is going to sell more papers, especially in the Western Cape. The fact that an auntie from Claremont's cat is trapped in a tree makes front page, while five people who die in a shack fire in Joe Slovo squatter camp is a small inside page story, is racism. Isn't it?

"I also think that the fact that people like you, Ryland, who have left the newspapers because of a sense of hopelessness and not being able to change things, indicates that there is still racism in the media."

"I think there is ignorance," said Obed. He said that he'd worked at Newspaper House when things were really racist. "Now they have a more diverse staff working there. I think the tendency is to ignore rather than be racist. I was angry when they ignored a story about a project in which I was involved in the townships. I thought they were racist, but then I realised that they were just ignoring people in the townships.

"I don't want to be judgemental or jump to conclusions. I have to have the facts before I can say that a group is racist. That is why I tend to use the word "ignorance". But they are spiting themselves by ignoring the townships. There are many professional people in the townships who read newspapers. There are people who actually go out of the township, over the highways and railway lines, to buy newspapers."

Leo insisted that the media was racist. "Maybe it is because of where I work or because of my political affiliation. But the fact that I work in the council and I see these fires and the next morning you open the papers and there is nothing, is frustrating. It is like, if it is not sensational, it's not worth it."

Leo suggested that all media should be forced to have a certain amount of educative information to deal with the issue of racism. "You tried to do it with the whole One City Many Cultures thing. I think the media should be forced to have a certain percentage of coverage that deals with the issue of racism. They should do this without having the need for 'racism police'.

Obed felt that there should not be separate editions of papers aimed at different constituencies, such as the townships. "There should only be one edition so that people can start seeing each other as one. They must also make more papers available in the townships."

Rhoda Kadalie

Rhoda Kadalie claimed that there was racism in the way the media reported on certain issues.

"Jane Raphaely [CEO of Associated Magazines] will tell you openly that when she has a black model on her cover, her sales drop dramatically. So they have white models on their magazine covers. This is in a country where black women are the majority. Isn't that ironic?"

I asked her whether racism was in the media or in the marketplace. "It is both in the media and the marketplace, because the media are the market.

"Many journalists are ignorant and are not even aware that they are racist in their reporting. They don't know how our value systems determine how we project certain stories.

"The media are racist in the way they report things, in the way they represent issues and the way they relegate certain stories to the back of the newspaper. The media is racist in the sense that white owners talk about empowerment, but their main concern is profits, and they put very little into training black journalists.

"The journalistic world is dominated by a layer of white men. The media is also very sexist. There are lots of women who could be editors of newspapers who are not even considered."

Asked what could be done about this, Rhoda said the answer lay in training. "Journalism schools should train people to identify racism and sexism. "All you need to do to prove that media is racist and sexist is to look at a month's worth of *Mail & Guardian*, *The Star*, and *Cape Times* editions, and analyse them. You also need to know what major events were happening in the country at the time.

"Chris Hani died at the time when there was a major storm in the country. The storm was the headline and not Chris Hani's assassination. Rugby will take priority over 30 people who are killed in a bus or train accident. That's the kind of stuff that smacks of racism."

Vincent Barnes

Vincent Barnes said that he had been a victim of racism in the media. "There are certain reporters I don't speak to. This is because of what they have written about me in the past.

"At Western Province, we had two coaches – myself and Eric Simons [who is white] – and the media always wrote about Eric's contribution. I got mentioned as a 'by the way'. Yet I was not assistant coach, but at the same level as Eric.

"The same thing happens on television. The television commentators act like I do not exist. They also have a full go at players of colour and promote the white players. I just put the sound off. Journalism is probably one of the most racist professions in South Africa."

Vincent said his response to racism in the media was to simply ignore certain people. "Some journalists have their own agendas. Sometimes I will speak to a journalist for more than half an hour and he will only use one line of what I have said. Yet others are fair and they don't promote any one particular person.

"The media intentionally mislead the public and they do it in such a way that the public will believe that the white man is running cricket in this province [Western Cape].

"I have said to my bosses that they must make it clear to the media that we have joint coaches here and that we must be given the same amount of coverage. If the media feel they need to praise one of us, both of us must be praised."

Naledi Pandor

Naledi Pandor defined the media as being guilty of double standards rather than racist. "Some people in South Africa were privileged under apartheid and did not see anything wrong with this. But if anyone else begins to have access to the kind of opportunities they had, they will call it affirmative action. I have a real problem with that and I see it particularly in the media in South Africa. I have not seen double standards of the nature that exist in our media anywhere else in the world. There is hardly any diversity in our media. You will find that stories are written in the same way in all our morning papers, and I feel horrified by that.

"Racism manifests itself in a lack of objectivity. It manifests itself in poor analysis and in assumptions."

Naledi also felt that there was a lot of incompetence which lead to bad reporting. "I think there is a lack of attention to detail, to an investigation of stories. There is a carelessness, which implies a double standard. For example, on the issue of Zimbabwe, there have been many reports that indicate that intimidation is practised by Zanu-PF and by the MDC. However, in the newspapers and on television, there is report after report which only refers to Zanu-PF violence. There is nothing about the MDC, so what is being conveyed is that only one party intimidates and practises violence. The other does not and yet there is clear evidence that both are guilty.

"Why are they reporting on the one and not the other? Is it the media's business to take up a position or to report? I believe the media in South Africa take up positions. I don't know if they report."

I asked whether this had to do with the colour of the government. "I used to think so, but now I am less convinced," she replied. "After observing this for a long time, I think it is just incompetence. It is a lack of professionalism. There are many young reporters working in the media. The mistakes are so basic as to suggest incompetence."

Asked what could be done about racism in the media, Naledi suggested: "We have to actively insist on professionalism. There are hardly any professional standards and surely that is one of the tasks of the editors. They need to pay special attention to ensuring that the people they employ are professional. For instance, when the rand declined, I thought the finance writers were going to investigate why this was happening, but nothing was investigated.

"When I lived in the States, you always had a fountain of information from journalists looking at the story behind the story, but we do not have this in South Africa."

Phatekile Holomisa
Phatekile Holomisa did not believe that racism was inherent in the media. "I think it has to do with culture. If, for instance, there were columns written in Xhosa or Zulu or Venda and so on, translated by Africans into English or Afrikaans, then whites would understand how these people think. We don't understand them and they don't understand us."

Carel Boshoff
"I know about the issues concerning racism in the media and the Human Rights Commission hearings, but I have not followed all the details," said Carel. "There are different newspapers with different perspectives. I don't know if it is racism when something is presented differently in some newspapers to other newspapers. If one looks at the whole issue of language presentation on state television, for instance, I get the impression that attempts to address racism can often have the

opposite effect.

"I am Afrikaans speaking and I often watch Afrikaans material on television. I would have been happy if there had been an Afrikaans channel on state television. Yet there are people who would see that desire of mine as a form of racism. If the debate around racism is premised on that kind of definition of racism, then I do not possess the ability to enter this debate."

Melanie Verwoerd

"The media is not racist, but there are individuals within the media who are racist," said Melanie. "With some writers you can feel the prejudice coming out in their writing. Journalists are supposed to be objective, but obviously they bring their personal stuff with them. Editors are supposed to watch out for that, but it is difficult. I don't think the media as an institution is racist, per se."

I asked her what could be done to counteract racism in the media, to which she replied, "Tough one. This is where government has to be very careful not to get too involved. I think civil society should play a much bigger role in terms of exposing racism in the media, objecting to it and even deciding not to buy certain media. Obviously faces in the media will have to change. Change has been very slow and I am surprised at this."

She pointed out that gender issues in the media had also been slow to change.

Athena and Manny Sotomi

Manny Sotomi felt that there was racism in the media, especially in the broadcast media. "I watched a programme where they showed children who had been abused," said Manny. "If it is a white child, they are very careful not to show the child's face. They will do everything in their power to cover it as much as possible. If it is a black child, you would recognise that child if you saw him or her on the street, because they cover the face up very half-heartedly. I think it is a form of racism when they do not take as much care in protecting the black kid as they do of the white kid. It has nothing to do with socio-economic status or anything else."

Asked what could be done about racism in the media, Manny said that black business people needed to buy the media or set up alternatives of a similar calibre. "If this happens, the newspapers with the racial bias will start to lose the market, because there is an alternative."

Athena felt differently. "That's one way of doing it. The other way is for people like you and me, when we see an incident like you described with the children, to actually make a noise about it, write to your ombudsman. Don't just sit there and complain; do something about it."

"You're right," said Manny. "It is all well and good theorising about it. But let's change it. Every little bit counts."

Tracy-Lee Rosslind

Tracy-Lee Rosslind believed racism manifested itself in stereotypes promoted in the media. "We need to get away from stereotypes, because the stereotypes that we had in the apartheid era all reflected negatively on the non-white society. Stereotypes are not true. There are certain racist stereotypes that get perpetuated in the media and we need to break away from them.

"On the television commercials, it is amazing how they use stereotypes. For instance, black people use Omo washing powder, while white people use Skip. They show black children running around with tyres. That is our reality, but it is only part of the reality.

"There are more than enough black children who go to Bishops [a formerly white private school] and Wynberg Boys' High [a formerly white public school]. They don't run around like those boys with the tyres. Why don't they show them?"

Asked what could be done about racism in the media, Tracy-Lee said: "We need to change the stereotypes. We need to show that we are all the same.

"I have been modelling for a few years now and the other day I went for a modelling shoot for a fashion house and they were looking for a coloured child. Everything has to be black, white and coloured. Previously it used to be white and coloured.

"They took me because I was fair and I wasn't too dark a coloured.

This is ridiculous. They took me because I didn't have straight hair but my hair is curly. We really need to break down these stereotypes. Something really should be done about it."

Kenny and Sielie Nolan
Sielie Nolan did not believe there was racism in the media. She felt that the broadcast media, for instance, was on the right track. "In the old days, only white people played roles on television. Nowadays when the news comes on, I sometimes complain that I can't understand when they speak African languages. But I understand that they were deprived of jobs in the media for so long, even though many of them are very talented."

Keathelia Satto
"I do not know enough about the media to say whether there is racism in it or not," said Keathelia. "From what I can see, it does not appear as if there is."

My thoughts

What is racism in the media? Is it racist to have pictures of only white people on your front pages? And is it racist to write about only white people? Is racism found in the way some media ignore certain sections of the population?

When I was editor of the *Cape Times*, my brief was to produce an "upmarket" newspaper. This meant that I had to aim at an audience with money, which my managers and staff thought meant white people.

Quite often, the news editor or a senior staff member would tell me about something that was happening in a black area, but they would also tell me that they were not going to cover it because it was happening outside our target market. I would respond by saying that, even though it was happening outside our target market, we still had to write about it, and in a way that would appeal to our target market.

The media are supposed to be a mirror on society, and one could argue that as long as our society is racist, the media will also be racist. However, I also believe that the media can play a leading role in determining and changing perceptions in society. Unfortunately, most media in South Africa do not seem to understand this role and continue to operate very much like they did in the apartheid days.

Until they realise the potential impact they have on society, it will be difficult to convince the media to change. But should the media fail to adapt, society will change regardless and reject them in the process. And that would prove disastrous not only for the media, but also for South Africa.

CHAPTER 10
CRITICISING GOVERNMENT: IS THIS RACISM?

Rainbow Man vs. Mr Delivery

After South Africans voted in our first democratic elections on 27 April 1994, there was a sense of euphoria throughout the country. Inspired by Nelson Mandela, South Africa also had two amazing sporting victories in the space of two years. We won the Rugby World Cup in 1995 and the African Cup of Nations soccer title the following year.

Since Mandela handed power over to Thabo Mbeki in 1999, people appear to be more critical of the government than before. Some people in government blame this increase in criticism on racism, particularly from white people. Those outside government generally accept that people are more critical today because they are allowed to be. Not too long ago, South Africa was still controlled by an apartheid regime that did not tolerate any alternative voices. Greater criticism of government is, in effect, one of the benefits of our freedom.

But the criticism of the Mbeki administration is also to be expected. Mbeki has to play a completely different role to the one played by Mandela. I wrote about this in an editorial in the *Cape Times* on 1 February 1999:

Mandela had to be the great unifier who tried to build a better understanding between blacks and whites. His role was

187

important given South Africa's past and the tenuous nature of our democracy.

Mbeki's role has to be different. If Mandela was the Rainbow Man, Mbeki has to be Mr Delivery. Mbeki is acutely aware of this and, in his victory speech yesterday, he emphasised that the mandate given to the ANC by an overwhelming majority of South Africans was to 'continue with the struggle for their upliftment and emancipation'.

He referred to 'the people' as being both black and white, and pledged to 'remain firm in the pursuit of our vision of a non-racial society and the important goal of national reconciliation'. But the emphasis was on work, as is typical of Mbeki. Unlike Mandela, who enjoys the public spotlight, Mbeki has a reputation as a workhorse.

But this is not without reason. Life for the majority of South Africans – the people who voted the ANC into power for a second term this week – has not changed much in the past five years.

Mbeki realises that he will have to speed up the transformation of our society. He has to improve the lives of the people who have placed their trust and confidence in his party. Otherwise they might not return him to power.

We do not envy Mbeki his enormous task and call on all South Africans, especially those in the minority parties, to help him deliver on his election promises. For the future of our country – and this is bigger than any one political party – it is important that Mbeki succeeds. We wish him well.

Mbeki is in a catch-22 situation. He has to deliver to the people who placed him in power. However, these are not the people, for instance, who have power over the media. So the more he delivers to his constituency, the more he runs the risk of upsetting the people who have the power over the media and other organs of society.

Mandela's response to criticism

But while it appears that people are more critical of Mbeki, they were also critical of Mandela's government. At some point during his presidency, Mandela got so upset with the media's criticism of the government that he launched a tirade against them, accusing the media of being controlled by whites, "in many cases conservative whites who are unable to reflect the aspirations of the majority".

At a meeting with Mandela, which I attended in June 1997 as part of a Sanef delegation, he said that many black journalists did not feel free to write what they wanted to write because of pressure from white editors.

Mandela repeated these comments at the ANC's 50th annual conference in Mafikeng in December 1997. He said that "during the last three years, the matter has become perfectly clear that the bulk of the mass media in our country has set itself up as a force opposed to the ANC."

He accused the media of campaigning against "both real change and the real agents of change" and decried a situation in which the "majority has no choice but to rely for information and communication on a media representing the privileged minority."

He accused the media of not hesitating to "denounce all efforts to ensure its own transformation, consistent with the objectives of a non-racial democracy, as an attack on press freedom".

He questioned the media's ability to deal with criticism. "When it speaks against us, this represents freedom of thought, speech and the press – which the world must applaud. When we exercise our own right to freedom of thought and speech to criticise it for its failings, this represents an attempt to suppress the freedom of the press – for which the world must punish us.

"Thus the media uses the democratic order, brought about by the enormous sacrifices of our own people, as an instrument to protect the legacy of racism, graphically described by its own patterns of ownership, editorial control, value system and advertiser influence.

"At the same time, and in many respects, it has shown a stubborn refusal to discharge its responsibility to inform the public."

Mandela said he was aware that his comments would be met "with a tirade of denunciation, with claims that what we are calling for is a media that acts as a 'lapdog' rather than a 'watchdog'".

He concluded by saying: "We ask for no favours from the media and we expect none. We make no apology for making the demand that the media has a responsibility to society to inform."

Mandela was applauded several times while he spoke about the role of the media. It was clear that the only people who were more unpopular than the media were "careerists and opportunists" who used the ANC for their own advancement.

I do not believe that politicians and the media will ever have a perfect relationship, but I feel that it is important to point out that there are also deficiencies in the media which affect the way they report on society.

I asked the people I interviewed whether they believed that there was racism in people's, and particularly the media's, criticism of government. The following are excerpts from their responses, again in no particular order.

Khusta and Karen Jack

Khusta Jack commented that people were more critical of the government today, but that this was not necessarily racism. "Racism is something else. The reason for the increase in criticism is because people can now express themselves freely. You are not going to be arrested for saying 'Mbeki is bad' or something like that. Anybody can say anything they like. There is no question of a restriction being imposed on you. That's a healthy situation. It is good for our country. It has nothing to do with the fact that the government is black.

Karen Jack, however, believed that there were white people who blamed corruption on the black government. "Many people cannot think about the causes of corruption and would just blame it on the black government. I am sure that there are many white people who do this."

Khusta agreed that there were more whites who were critical of government than blacks. "That's a strange phenomenon. Before, white people in general were not critical, because they saw no need to be and not because of the fear of being repressed. Things were good for them and they didn't care about what was happening. They could have criticised the government and that would not have landed them in trouble. White people have always had a history of voting, electing and being involved in government.

"The government now has to contend with a body of criticism coming from all facets of society. Many of the criticisms are not necessarily wrong, though. Most of them are constructive, bringing to the government's attention things that ought to be fixed."

Karen interjected: "People need to be reminded that our country has never been as good as it is today."

I pointed out that I have noticed that most of the black columnists in newspapers were largely negative towards the government and that you could hardly find a black columnist who was positive about South Africa. Khusta proposed that part of the reason for this was because the government under Nelson Mandela antagonised black intellectuals.

"The government undermined them in every way. Many of these guys moved back into academia and forgot about being involved in anything that had to do with attempting to help the country.

"The other problem is that the majority of the people who stood up in the debate to influence South Africa's agenda in the past, are all in government. Therefore they are now restricted by official protocols.

"So who are you going to find now to write for the papers? It is just these chaps who were not involved in the struggle. Many of them became so-called doctors, but they are our age. You have to wonder how they became doctors. While we were struggling, they were getting an education. Therefore their education is half-baked in terms of the South African situation."

Trevor Oosterwyk

Trevor Oosterwyk reckoned there should be a long public debate around the question of whether people had become more critical of the government because it was black.

"It is a beautiful question and one that must be opened up for a public debate. I have been thinking about this question a lot," he said. "We cannot be seen to be too critical of this government, and if we are going to say that Mbeki is messing up big time, are we buying into this notion that blacks can't govern?

"People say, 'Look at the rest of Africa, they messed up everywhere they went.' Are we then selling that idea? If we are bent upon just exposing the negatives of this government, are we reinforcing this notion that blacks can't rule? People will say things like 'they are corrupt', 'they are backward', 'they can't govern', and 'they mess up everything'. This kind of criticism has built up over many years.

"I am often asked to act as a commentator on public issues and I always worry how much of what I say is genuinely what I believe in, or whether I am buying into this belief that one must just criticise government. If I do that, to what extent am I reinforcing this whole notion that black people cannot rule? It is such a complex question. We must be critical of corruption, for example, but we must also say where government is doing the right thing.

"What I am saying is that I think there must be a carefulness about criticising until we have built enough of a foundation in society to prove that black people can govern. South Africa is still too young to make judgments as to whether black people can govern or not. We cannot perpetuate that notion."

Vincent Barnes

Vincent Barnes believed that people were more critical of the government because it was black. "White people still live exactly where they lived before, and they do exactly what they did before. They have lost nothing except that they no longer sit alone. They have to sit with black people. They will always find a problem with black people in power, because when there were no black people in power, everything was hunky-dory.

"It is sad every time you read about the government or about the United Cricket Board – it is negative because the president of the country is black and the CEO of the cricket board is black. The cricket board gets an unnecessary amount of criticism in the media. It seems like many people in the media long for the days when the cricket board was run by white people.

"Whenever Percy Sonn [the president of the cricket board at the time of the interview] does anything different, it gets highlighted in the media. In the old days, people were allowed to make mistakes and could get away with it."

Carel Boshoff

"Everyone knows that it is not good manners to explicitly and expressly criticise the government because it is black," said Carel. "Those people who criticise the government because it is black do it in a suspect manner."

"There is a heightened kind of criticism of government. But to my experience, there was a less critical attitude towards the transitional government of Mr Mandela than there has been to the transformational government of Mr Mbeki. There are reasons for this. Transition is always easier than transformation. It is meant to be easier than transformation and this has a hell of an impression on the way people react to it. Transformation touches people's lives, it touches their work, and it touches their expectations of the future.

"The problem is that, to my experience and in the circles in which I move, there are many people who, in principle, are very positive about the changes that must happen. But when it really begins to touch their lives, then they become critical and this can often be translated into racism.

"My problem is that if the government starts protecting itself against criticism by using the race card, then there is a risk that they will avoid criticism completely. It is probably a bit idealistic, but I would love to have a government that incorporates criticism rather than rejects it."

Phatekile Holomisa

"There are instances where you would believe there is more criticism because the government is black," said Phatekile. "For instance, a lot of people in the countryside, if they do not get the services they are entitled to, will say that things were better during the time of apartheid. 'Even if the *umlungu* treated us badly and regarded us as inferior, we at least got the services,' they say. 'We got what we needed, we were employed. We were getting health services and things like that, even though not all the services were rendered.' They will say this in innocence, and not because blacks are unable to manage their affairs.

"The media is always controlled by whites and they have their own values and their own culture, and this has to come through in reports that you find in the newspaper. They don't understand the way blacks have to do certain things, even while in government. For instance, there is this question of a need for consultation. Some government projects aimed at bettering the lives of the people were being rejected in the rural areas, because of the manner in which they were introduced. You need to consult a lot of people to make them understand, and allow them to ask questions and come forward with their own views, before you can implement anything.

"Some of the provisional services tend to be delayed even though there is an urgent need for these services, because at the same time there is a need for proper consultation. Then newspapers will highlight the results of the inaction and say that government is failing to do this and that, because they don't understand the process that government has to go through.

"Of course, other writers, reporters and editors are black themselves, and they understand what is happening, but they have to adapt to the [white] value system at the newspapers."

Rhoda Kadalie

"When people criticise this government, I am convinced that they are racists, but what I am sad about is that we prove these racists to be correct.

"Thabo Mbeki is powerful. He must lead with conviction and not as a victim. He insists on being the victim, on playing the race card. This is what troubles me, that they [the government] will continually evoke the past to justify the present.

"Thabo must lead with confidence. When people don't lead with confidence, they will resort to all kinds of excuses to justify their mistakes.

"There are racists [who criticise the government], but I also think that Africa is a basket case and proves the racism of the world right. That is what saddens me. We in South Africa can be the definitive democracy, but we are increasingly behaving like the 'tin pots' of Africa. I watch Nepad [the New Partnership for Africa's Development] closely and we have people talking about African standards of democracy. What they are saying is that there's a Western concept of democracy and there's an African concept of democracy. This is a lot of rubbish."

Naledi Pandor

"When I read media reports, they always give the impression that there is very limited activity by government," said Naledi. "The media only reports on the President's view or someone else's view and not on what is being done by government.

"I would have expected the media to have gone out and actually said, 'We have investigated and this is what's happening on the ground.' People say things like 'there were four million South Africans who are affected by Aids', but who are the four million people? How did we identify them and what is the nature of their illness? This lack of depth, this taking up of positions, is, for me, a problem in relation to the media."

Wilmot James

"When the ANC won in 1994 and they established a majority government, a lot of people, especially (but not only) white people, saw this as a new government controlled by black people inexperienced in the art of running a government. That made them worry, especially given the so-called record of African governments."

"They were pleasantly surprised by Nelson Mandela and his first Cabinet, which were a good group of people. The first five or six years of democratic rule were extraordinary. They had to establish a new government and resolve all kinds of conflicts, and if you consider where they came from, they did not do too badly. In fact, they exceeded most people's expectations.

"There came a stage when many people were realising that a lot of it had to do with Mandela and his growing stature. Since Mandela left, there has been some continuity in government, but there is a sense that after the first five years, the government is not doing as well as it should be doing, for whatever reasons.

"Part of the assumption for this situation is that the government is black. I do think this perception exists and that our government has to prove itself ten times more than a normal government.

"There are big problems out there, such as HIV/Aids and crime, but the achievements have been extraordinary. For instance, around the issue of fiscal and monetary management, there has been a first-class approach. Education and trade and industry are also doing exceptionally well. A lot of this is spoilt by the President's lack of clarity around HIV/Aids.

"But the assumption in civil society that black people really cannot govern is probably still there and this often informs how the media responds as well. And if black people can govern properly, then that is really wonderful and exceptional. It is not taken as the norm."

Melanie Verwoerd

Melanie Verwoerd agreed that some people were more critical of the government because it was black. "Again, it is some people and not all people. I have this constant argument with people because they base their arguments on presumptions. I find this often among white people.

"The Observer Mission comes back from Zimbabwe with a qualified report and the assumption is that the black government was going to support Mugabe no matter what. People do not look at whether there is any truth in what the Observer Mission might have said.

"This irritates me, these assumptions based on race. I think our communities play a role in this and we have largely been segregated. The media also plays a role. However, I don't know if this is racism. It depends on who the criticism is coming from, what is being said and how it is being said."

Athena and Manny Sotomi

"I think it is a good thing if people, and especially the media, are critical of the government," said Manny. "Constructive criticism is good, and if the media do their research properly before they criticise, and ask pertinent questions, this will make our politicians accountable. That is what, in my view, journalism is about: telling people the truth."

196

Tracy-Lee Rosslind

Tracy-Lee Rosslind said that there was definitely racism in many people's criticisms of the government.

"At my school, I often hear comments that the government is in place because they are black. The children also make comments like, 'They come straight out of Standard Three [Grade Five] and they go straight into government.'

"There was a cartoon that came out just before the government came into power and it showed all these people who did not know what they were doing. The only black politician that is looked upon as someone with any sense is Nelson Mandela, who is my hero. But he is definitely not the only black person who has done something for this country.

"I agree with Thabo Mbeki on the whole Aids story. He is right. He has to look out for the well-being of the entire country. Just because everybody says that something is true does not mean that they are right. AZT was proven absolutely unhealthy when it came into this country. So how can he take the risk of putting all his people in this country under that kind of danger? Just because America, which is seen as this amazing power, says it is right, does not mean it is right.

"We need to get out of this belief that the United States is God-sent and that everybody else is wrong. We need to start being proud of South Africa and proud that we are African."

Leo de Souza and Obed Zilwa

Leo de Souza stressed that criticism of any government was important for democracy. "Everybody has a responsibility to look at the government, to agree and disagree. That is not only your right, but your responsibility. However, if you have a planned and thought-out path to criticise the government, to break them down, to break down issues of progress and transformation, then I have a problem with that.

"I suspect that there is a plot and there is a group of people who use the media and their political connections to do that.

"The other important thing is not to refer to the government as a black government. It is our government. There might be a black president, but it is our government."

Kenny and Sielie Nolan

According to Kenny, people were more critical of the new government, because it was black. "Many things went wrong in the past and the old government did many bad things. The people who are now in government opposed the old government for many years. But the old government was a white government; now that there is a black government, many people are again finding reasons to complain."

Keathelia Satto

Keathelia Satto argued that people's criticism of the government was not a matter of racism: "People would have criticised them anyway, even if they were white."

My thoughts

On 19 October 1977, the South African government banned the *World* and *Weekend World* newspapers, along with several journalists, some of whom were imprisoned.

South Africa has come a long way since the days when the government responded to criticism in one way only: through repression. But how does the ANC government respond to criticism, and has the criticism become more vocal because there is now a black government in place or because there is now a democratic government in place?

In a country such as South Africa, where race has for so long been a part of our soul, it is difficult not to see a racist agenda behind just about everything in society. Yet there is an advantage to this vigilant focus on the subject of racism: hopefully it will also serve as a constant reminder of our past and a warning that we should never go down that road again.

Criticism of a democratic government is to be expected because people feel more free to criticise. Even the biggest critics of government will appreciate the fact that they are now free to raise their criticism without fear of repression or victimisation.

There is probably a lot of merit in Leo De Souza's point about not referring to South Africa's government as a black government. Maybe when all South Africans feel able to call the government "our government", we will have made some progress in terms of limiting the amount of criticism directed at the government.

CHAPTER 11
IS THERE STILL A NEED FOR EXCLUSIVELY BLACK (OR WHITE) ORGANISATIONS?

'Verwoerd would have been proud of you'

In 1999, I addressed the annual gala dinner of the Black Management Forum (BMF) in the Western Cape. As editor of the *Cape Times*, I supported the BMF, and the *Cape Times* had become a co-sponsor of the BMF annual gala dinner.

I explained why I supported the BMF, which was an organisation targeting mainly black professionals, and why I felt that a need for such an organisation existed.

My view was that as long as there remained inequalities in our society, we would need to have organisations to campaign almost exclusively on behalf of black people. Survey after survey showed that whites still got most of the top jobs in South Africa, and that blacks had not benefited from policies like affirmative action in the way that people claimed they had. While non-racial organisations were to be encouraged, I could understand completely the need for black people to congregate in their own organisations, where they could discuss their problems with people who understood their situation.

I explained that while there was a need for a black management forum, I did not feel there was any need for a white management forum, because white people did not need to deal with the inequalities created by apartheid.

I published my speech in the *Cape Times* and got severely criticised by a columnist from the *Mail & Guardian*, who said that Hendrick Verwoerd, the father of apartheid, would have been proud of me. He said that where I had used the word "black", Verwoerd had simply used "white".

A few months later, I spoke to this columnist on the telephone. It was the first time that we had spoken, and he ended up inviting me to his farm somewhere in the Western Cape. I think I convinced him that I was not a "Verwoerd" and that we should at least talk about issues such as the transformation of South African society.

It has been several years since 1999, but sadly the situation has not changed much in South Africa. Black people are still under-represented in senior management positions and economic power remains in white hands. Consequently, there is still a need for organisations targeting black people. I hope the day will come when we will no longer require such organisations, but I fear this need will exist for many more years.

I asked the people I interviewed whether they felt there was still a need for exclusively black organisations in South Africa. The following are some of their answers, again in no particular order.

Carel Boshoff

Carel Boshoff reasoned that the irony of having black organisations today was that if they had been exclusively white, they would have provoked a stronger reaction. "If you start a white students' organisation or a white personnel union on a university campus, it will definitely provoke a strong reaction, while no one will think twice if a black caucus exists on the same campus," he said.

"Of course there are historic reasons for this. This is a group that mobilises to promote its own interests. From the outside it looks a bit strange and I would be inclined to say, can't we now move on beyond that point? Can't we just move on to a point where people choose to belong [to organisations] and are not excluded because they are not black? It makes me feel uncomfortable, but I am careful not to be prescriptive about something of which I do not have first-hand experience."

Rhoda Kadalie

Rhoda Kadalie did not agree that there was a need for exclusively black organisations such as the Black Management Forum. "They have achieved what they wanted to achieve. The Black Management Forum has now become a mouthpiece for the ruling elite. So what is the purpose of that organisation? The purpose was to bring together black management expertise and talk about how to empower them in terms of the job market. We now have a new South Africa and there is a huge sector of powerful black managers in our country.

"I still believe that a women's organisation should exist, given the epidemic of violence against women, discrimination against women, and so on.

"You need to look at the contexts in order to justify the existence of exclusive groups. But I find organisations based on race very problematic. If I wanted to start a white women's group that would concentrate on the development of Crossroads, however, that would be different. That would be a public interest group that acknowledges they are privileged, that they are white, that they are wealthy and that they want to work towards development. I am not against groupings and formations per se. I am against people who group around race for race's sake.

"The Black Management Forum has to make a case to me as to why they want to exist and I will weigh up the argument."

Wilmot James

"There are sometimes circumstances where people have to group together on the basis of a common set of experiences in order to stand firm and to enhance their ability to compete in the general marketplace," explained Wilmot. "That's a judgement call. I don't see anything wrong with that and I think it can be quite valuable if there is a general understanding that this is necessary.

"In the US, they have the Black Congressional Caucus. No one thinks it is a bad thing to have and it adds enormous value to policy making in the US."

I pointed out that South Africa was different to the US because we had a black majority whereas they had a black minority. Some people would argue that for this reason there was no need for exclusively black organisations.

"The black majority controls the state," he responded. "The black majority does not control the economy."

Naledi Pandor

"I am worried about the current direction we seem to be taking, which appears to suggest that we may not even have historically black institutions of higher learning. People's sense of self is shaped as much by the milieu as by the institutions that represent them or reflect them. I don't think that historically black institutions would necessarily reflect badly on me, Naledi, as an African.

"I think what's problematic is this attitude that black people cannot successfully manage an institution of higher learning. Getting rid of these institutions to me implies that black people do not have the capacity to run them. That is how I would read it and this makes me very worried.

"I believe there is a need for black institutions and organisations. Black institutions can focus on issues from a black perspective. Anybody can belong, but it means that you have a strong grouping of black people who are able to define the direction and the function of that institution or organisation. I am probably a maverick in this view, but that is what I think."

Phatekile Holomisa

Phatekile Holomisa found the question difficult to answer because, he explained, "Nowadays there is freedom of association in South Africa. I know that there are clan groupings that formed themselves into some societies. For instance, people who are still based in rural areas, working in the labour centres, will group themselves as members of that clan in order to help each other if there is a wedding or *ngidi* (a coming of age of ceremony) or if there's a funeral. In this way they are able to help each other. Naturally, those groupings will be black and they will be speaking the same language, because they belong mostly to the same clan. There's nothing wrong with that. It does not threaten anyone.

"With regard to the corporate world, it is important for people who have similar problems to be able to sit down and share their problems, share their experiences and share the solutions that they have found. But it should not be in order to perpetuate that exclusiveness. It should be in order to facilitate entry into the other areas that we don't have access to, because of a lack of resources, and skills and training that was denied to us. It should be seen as moving towards a much more open society, to strategise in order to be able to be together.

"For instance, women have many grievances against society and they can't successfully fight against those grievances if they don't give themselves the opportunity to sit down and share and strategise, with a view to gaining access and overcoming problems. It should be a means to an end rather than an end itself."

Melanie Verwoerd

Melanie said she felt uncomfortable about exclusively black organisations. "It's not only about race. It's about other issues, too. I remember going to America and feeling really irritated by their Black Caucus, but at the same time we have a women's caucus," she said.

"I think it depends on how the organisation operates, what it does and what its intentions are. But I am inherently uncomfortable with exclusive organisations, because their intentions may be really good to start off with, but the way they are perceived from the outside and the effects that they have are often very different. For example, in America today, it has become very tough for people who are not African-American to become part of the social movement, because it has become a very exclusive movement.

"We need to be careful. I understand that it is about getting power, about being able to discuss common issues and about being able to mobilise and reach joint strategies, but when it becomes exclusive, it becomes dangerous."

Trevor Oosterwyk

Trevor Oosterwyk was ambivalent about the need for exclusively black organisations. "If one asks the question, one is suggesting that there must come a time when there should not be a need for these organisations, but I think that maybe we will always need organisations like this. I just think that when we do have organisations like this, we tend to talk among each other and reinforce some of the negative notions we have.

"If we have organisations that are more open, we tend to get ideas that do not reinforce one side or one set of ideas. There's a greater cross-fertilisation. Ultimately, I would aim for the establishment of open, free organisations based on the free association of people.

"I still see the necessity for people who have a common history and experience to come together and determine their contribution and judgement."

Leo de Souza and Obed Zilwa

Leo de Souza and Obed Zilwa agreed that there was no longer any need for exclusively black organisations.

"Black people also need to learn to be inclusive," said Leo. "That doesn't mean that you are taking away power. If you want to build power, it is fine. If you want to strengthen yourself, it is fine, but don't do it to the exclusion of any other party. One of my biggest problems is what will happen if white people did it [formed exclusive organisations], or if coloured people did it. It would just lead to greater exclusiveness.

"I believe we should be guided by Madiba's speech about opposing white domination and black domination. The content of the issue is important and it should focus on black issues and empowerment, but not exclude them. We had organisations such as the Broederbond, which looked exclusively at certain issues, and they became exclusive clubs which empowered only certain people. We must not fall in that trap again."

Obed agreed. "I don't know what these organisations stand for, whether they are there to fight for jobs or to ensure that black people in business are ultimately protected. If they look at the whole issue of black people as part of management, then there might be a need, but I am not sure.

"Some people might think that I am sympathising with white people, and maybe I am, but I cannot agree with apartheid in reverse."

Khusta and Karen Jack

Khusta Jack felt that there was still a need for exclusively black organisations, but only to a limited extent. "There is an unfinished job to close the gap between black and white. People who think that the management structures in the country ought to be changed, have to participate in some form of a group, whether you call it the Black Management Forum or something else. We need an organisation that will work to advance black managers and to make sure that black people are represented in the top structures of business."

Keathelia Satto

Keathelia Satto did not see a need for exclusively black organisations. "I think it is wrong for these organisations to exist. How can we stop racism if they continue to exclude people on the basis of race?"

My thoughts

Exclusively black organisations have their roots in the apartheid days when there was a need for a united black response to white supremacy. As such, many organisations with "black" in their titles were formed. The argument, rightly or wrongly, was that white people were united in their oppression of black people and it was important for black people to be united against white supremacy.

After the abolition of apartheid, there was a feeling that the inequalities that started under apartheid would take a long time to overcome and that black people needed to be united in their attempts to overcome these inequalities.

As long as most of the senior positions in South African corporates are occupied by white men, and most black people continue to be at the bottom rung of society's ladder, there will probably remain a need for blacks-only organisations within the business environment. This need will only change once there are no longer discrepancies between blacks and whites, and blacks, too, have economic power.

CHAPTER 12
HOW DO WE EXPLAIN APARTHEID TO OUR YOUTH?

'There you go again, dad'

A while ago I went to a funeral of an old ANC activist in Mitchells Plain, a suburb of Cape Town. There were many people at this funeral, including some government ministers and the then mayor of Cape Town. I took my older daughters, then aged about 14 and 12, with me to the funeral and afterwards they asked me how it was that I knew most of the people there. I explained that we had all been involved in the struggle. I asked whether they knew what "the struggle" was, and my middle daughter said it had something to do with apartheid and racism.

I realised then that our struggle against apartheid means very little to our children. I have tried several times in the past few years to talk to my daughters about apartheid and the struggle, but every time I am told "There you go again, Dad" or "Not again, Dad".

In some ways, their attitude is encouraging in that it reflects that they are no longer worried about the issues that we used to worry about. But it could also mean that they are not concerned about the struggle and about apartheid and this could have implications for our future. Many years after the Holocaust happened in Germany, it is still fresh in people's memories and young people are reminded of it all the time. Some would argue that apartheid was as big a crime against humanity and needs to be remembered in the same way.

But there is hope in the way that young people respond to racism. It has become very clear to me that racism is not something we are born with, but something that we get taught. One day I was at my youngest daughter's school and we were looking for a particular boy. I asked one of the little girls to point him out to me. She pointed to a group of boys and told me that he was the one wearing a blue shirt. He was the only black boy in the group, but she identified him by the colour of the shirt he was wearing and not by the colour of his skin.

In her autobiographical book *Our Generation*, Zubeida Jaffer wrote about how she introduced race to her daughter at a protest against segregated beaches in the late 1980s, and described her daughter's reaction.

Ruschka has become aware that my mind is not with her and is tired of the game I pretend to be playing. She is tugging at me to take her onto the beach so that she can go into the water. She is a child who makes a beeline for the sea whenever we visit. Johnny, all his children and myself had this one thing in common. We all loved the water and took to it like fishes. In the summer months, swimming was our main recreational activity.

We are expecting Archbishop Tutu to arrive to head the protest but he has in the meantime been advised to make a detour to Bloubergstrand, a beach on the West Coast to which protestors are being redirected. Ruschka keeps on tugging and demands why she cannot go into the water.

"Those men with the dogs don't want us to go into the water, Ruschka."

"Why, mummy, why?"

I don't know what to say. I suddenly realise that this child has no idea of race. I have never introduced her to the concept and how do I now explain to her that she cannot go into the water because this is a white beach and that she is not white. I do not want to do it. For so long our central passion has been building a non-racial society where all of us can just be human beings, not punished for the colour of our skin.

She is insisting. What should I say?

I swallow hard. "Well, Ruschka, you can't go into the water because you are not white."

For a moment, she is still, as if pondering what I have said. I am relieved that the tugging has stopped. Then she looks down at her white track-top and grips it with two fingers, pulling it away from her body. "But, mommy, I am white."

I asked my interviewees how we should explain apartheid to our youth and how we could prevent it from happening again. I also asked them whether it was possible to teach young people anti-racist values.

Tracy-Lee Rosslind

"Without a past, you cannot have a present and you cannot have a future," said Tracy-Lee.

"We need to educate people on what happened, because everybody has amnesia. Once we forget, the same thing can happen again – which is going to become a problem, because everybody is forgetting.

"I don't believe in forgiving and forgetting. You can forgive, but if you have forgotten what you have actually forgiven, then that is a problem. You don't remember what you have forgiven, so you can make the same mistake over and over and nothing gets done about it.

"We need to educate the youth about what happened. We need to show them what happened, what is being done about it and how the country is today.

"Let me give you an example. The education system was terrible. The people were taught absolutely nothing that they could use in their lives. Today it is being brought to a level where we will all have the same opportunities and we will all be able to do the same jobs, to the best of our abilities."

"It is possible to teach young people anti-racist values, but it involves more work than most people are willing to do. If you learn from young that something is wrong or something is right, and you grow up believing that, then you will teach those same beliefs to your children. Youth can be taught what is right and what is wrong. But you need to give them facts and it is very difficult to prove to somebody that their parents were wrong, when their parents are their first role models. You actually need to start teaching them and drilling into their heads that it is fine not to be racist, that black is not wrong. Black people are not the enemy and we can all live together in harmony.

"Sport can also play a major role. When our national team won the Rugby World Cup, you could not believe the unity in the country. Even when South Africa was playing at the Soccer World Cup, you would find white families watching. And soccer is supposed to be a black game in South Africa.

"But it is important not to keep drilling, otherwise it will become an old issue. When people talk to the youth about the past without showing them what happened, it just goes in the one ear and out the other."

Keathelia Satto
I asked Keathelia Satto what apartheid was. "What I have learnt about apartheid is that all the white people lived on one side of the road and all the black people lived on the other side. They were not allowed to communicate with each other."

I asked her what could be done to prevent apartheid from happening again. "They should not allow only white people to get certain jobs," she replied. "They must allow other colours, and other races to also get the same jobs."

I asked her whether it was possible to teach young people anti-racist values. "Yes. You need to teach them to understand other people's views and not just base their views of people on colour."

Trevor Oosterwyk
"Apartheid cannot be explained in simple terms, because it has never been that simple. The history of 1948 started probably in the 14th century. By the time 1948 came and happened, there was a powerful military regime in place that was probably among the top three in the world at the time.

"There were also people who had been militarily, politically and socially defeated, slowly, over many years, including the Khoi, the Xhosa, the Zulu and the Tswana.

"On the other hand, there was a military might that was there to enforce whatever decisions had been made. That was the beauty of it all. It could police and enforce its laws. It could drive into a community with its trucks and move the people. But it was not only that. It was also the destruction of the ability to build up an alternative power force to challenge it.

"It was single-minded about destroying, as long as it could, any military challenge to its rule, any force that was capable of challenging it. It did it for a long time, for 50 years.

"At the same time, one has to say, it was not always that successful. It was not as if they had carte blanche. All through our history there was resistance, from small uprisings to major activities of revolutionary proportions. This happened all the time and apartheid could never completely successfully keep us all under the thumb. That was the downfall, but it did manage to create a life of 50 years for itself in the process.

"If you look at history, then 50 years is nothing, and then one must say it failed. Apartheid failed because it could not last for longer than 50 years. Something like the Roman Empire lasted for many years longer. So, if we talk about apartheid in the greater sense of history, it was not successful.

"Apartheid, in the form of white superiority or black superiority, has died and won't be resuscitated, because no one person will ever again have the physical strength to enforce such an idea. The world has moved further down the line and we won't allow apartheid to happen again, in the same way that a Hitler will never be able to rise to kill the Jews again. The world will not allow it to happen again, because it happened already.

"The fact that there might, in South Africa, arise a minority who controls the majority, is possible. The only thing we can do to ensure it does not happen is to fight for the maintenance and the deepening of democracy. We need to use all our instruments to do this, including the media, and education, education, education. We need to develop a diversity of ideas and critically-minded citizens.

"I think that teaching young people anti-racist values is not only possible, but the single most important responsibility of all human beings in a society that has been wrecked by racism, and where some of those ideas are so dominant.

"We have to teach our kids about all forms of prejudice, particularly colour prejudice and hair prejudice. We need to deal with that when it comes to our children. Our houses need to be the first places where we act when we hear our children talk about Kaffirs or Boere or whatever.

"Our schools also have to run anti-racist programmes. We need a national curriculum that teaches anti-racist values. But we should not harp on about anti-racism. We should rather teach morals and ethics of tolerance. We should teach children about patriotism, and that we all belong together and nobody is better than anybody else. We should teach children from a very young age that there is no big difference between races. We are all just people."

Leo de Souza and Obed Zilwa

"We have to tell our youth the truth about apartheid. It happened and we cannot get away from that. It is our responsibility to let children know what happened. I am worried that we are losing this. We have not been keeping proper records and we are so into the rainbow nation that we are forgetting about the horrors of apartheid, and we can't do that."

Obed Zilwa felt that the best way to prevent apartheid from happening again was to talk about it. "We need to talk about it in our schools, at our workplaces and in our communities. Knowing each other is the best way to prevent apartheid happening again."

Leo used a story involving Obed's son to illustrate that it was possible to teach young people anti-racist values. "Obed and I had been dating and we took Thando, who was four at the time, on some dates with us. We had known each other for about three weeks and we were driving in Obed's car when Thando suddenly stood up and, looking at me very strangely, said: 'Hey daddy, isn't Leo white?' After three weeks, he had suddenly realised that I was white. I think somebody probably asked him that question, because it did not matter to him before then.

"He also came to us and asked whether Nikki, our baby, was a Muslim. I asked him how Nikki could be a Muslim if we were Christians. I realised then that to him, coloured people are Muslims and he saw Nikki as being a coloured person. He went to school in Walmer Estate, which is a predominantly coloured Muslim area, so he assumed that all coloureds were Muslim.

"We discuss these issues with the boys. They see themselves as black. However, at one stage Thando told people in the townships that he was white, because his mommy was white. I am white, so he is white.

"When we sat them down and explained apartheid to them, they were shocked. They could not understand. The biggest shock to them was that we could not use the same toilet. This was the most important fact to them, and not the fact that people were killing each other. When we ask them what apartheid is, they say it is when one person tries to hurt another person. It is not an issue of colour to them. It is about instilling proper values in them. We have to be open about these things.

"Xhabiso gave a speech in Afrikaans about '*my familie*'. He showed them pictures and said 'this is my father, this is my mother, this is my brother' and so on. Then he said, in Afrikaans, '*Julle dink seker dat ons is anders, maar ons is ni*e [You probably think we are different, but we are not].'

"He said, 'We eat the same food, we drink the same drinks, we play in the same way, I go to the same school as you, and we are all the same.'

"So, yes, I think you can instill values of non-racialism in children, but it has to be on the basis of respect for people."

Obed continued. "They came home one day from the township, talking about 'makwerrie kwerries' [*amakwerekwere*], referring to illegal aliens. I hated this, but I told them why it was wrong to call people names like that and they understood. They surprise us from time to time, but we try to explain things to them so that when they grow up they will understand that there is no need for them to treat other people differently."

Leo said members of the public tended to ask the boys questions about their heritage. "We would go to Pick 'n Pay and the till packers would look at me and then speak to the boys in Xhosa. They would ask them things like 'So, does your mother work for this lady?' and they would reply 'no'. Then they would ask 'Are you adopted?' and still the answer would be 'no'. The boys would then say that I was their mother. The till packers would then ask them where they lived and other questions like that. The boys deal with this all the time. When you pick them up at school, the children quickly notice that there is a white mommy and ask them about it."

I asked what language they speak to the children at home. "We speak mainly English to them, but there are Xhosa influences. Obed speaks a lot of Xhosa to the boys," said Leo.

"I can honestly say," said Obed, "that we teach our children that there are no differences between people. Whether you are white or black, we are all the same."

Melanie Verwoerd

"One has to explain apartheid to our youth as honestly as possible. Knowledge, knowledge, knowledge: that is the key. We need to keep on talking about it, we have to have feelings about it, we have to have documentaries about it, and we have to have plays about it."

She cited an example of her daughter, who was then 11, choosing to do a school project on apartheid. "She has always known about apartheid. We have always told her about it and she understands. She always saw it as an economic issue, for instance the shacks in Khayamandi [a township] versus the nice houses in Stellenbosch.

"After she watched a video on the Truth Commission, she was very, very clear about it. We had huge family discussions after that, and the Verwoerd issue became a huge issue in our family. So we had long discussions about that.

"We need to debate, and we need to talk about apartheid so that it can be in the consciousness of our children. That is the only way we can prevent apartheid from happening again."

Melanie believed it was possible to teach young people anti-racist values. "It is an absolute necessity. And it is not only about racism. It is also about culture and religion and about other differences between people. We moved to Cape Town from Stellenbosch in 1996 because it was incredibly difficult in Stellenbosch. We sent our children to St George's Grammar School, which had a mixture of children from different religions, but especially Muslims.

"Wilmien had a hat that she only wore on special occasions. She just loved that hat. One day she put it on before she went to school and I asked her what the occasion was. She said it was Eid and asked me whether I did not know that.

"Another interesting thing happened just after September 11. Wilmien was 12. One day she came home, distraught. I asked her what had happened at school and she said that people were saying that Muslim people were terrorists. She had tears in her eyes and said she'd had a huge argument at school. She said she told the children at school that she knows Muslim people and they are not terrorists. She told them her friends in Cape Town were Muslims. In a way it was tough on her, but I felt that she was privileged to be able to make distinctions that not even adults could make.

"People often ask me whether I will return to South Africa and I say, 'Of course.' Then they say, 'What about your children?' and I say, 'It's because of my children.' I want my children to be raised in a multicultural society. It is a tremendous privilege to have this multicultural society in South Africa."

Carel Boshoff

Asked how one would explain apartheid to our youth, Carel Boshoff said: "I would explain it in terms of the idea of categorical discrimination, meaning that it did not affect individuals, but categories of people, and that people's individuality was subservient to these categories.

"I would explain that discrimination happened in this sense and that it was unreasonable, because it happened in the light of these categories, instead of judging people by their individual abilities or merits. To prevent this would require that power should be held in a better equilibrium.

"The risk we run at the moment is to have an oppressive majority that will simply ignore the wishes of certain minority categories and groups, and that the choice that people have in terms of their own identities will be subjected to new categories. This is where you have the danger of maybe not a new apartheid, but a new form of oppression, a new form of categorical discrimination."

I asked him whether it was possible to teach young people anti-racist values. "I think it is possible if we do two things," he answered. "The one is to impress on young people that you are always dealing with individuals. Each person should be approached with an open attitude. Eventually you might decide that a person is clever or stupid, but you owe him a chance, because in the first place he is an individual and cannot be reduced to some marker of his identity, especially not a racial identity.

"But one also has to look at the social conditions under which people are comfortable to treat someone as an individual. When my group or my community does not feel threatened, I can be very accommodating and tolerant of others. When the opposite happens – when, for instance, my religious beliefs are oppressed by the state, for example if I were a Muslim – then this calls up a lot of aggression that is difficult to suppress. In this way, a child can enjoy a certain amount of security in his own community. He will not feel threatened and will develop a sense of the individuality in all people."

Phatekile Holomisa

"The best way to explain apartheid to the youth is to relate the story just the way it happened, as part of history. The children should be taught what used to happen, so that they understand the silliness of it all, the inhumanness of it. How could people created by the same God, in His image, treat others in the way whites treated blacks in this country?

"It is important that this story be told and be taught as part of our history. At the same time, they need to be told of the transformation that has taken place, so that they can appreciate the sacrifices that were made by those who fought for it, now that they are able to mingle with their peers of whatever racial group, without any restriction. I think the answer is education.

"I would not necessarily teach young people anti-racist values as such. I would just teach them to understand that a human being is a creature of God and you have to treat people in the way you want them to treat you. One of my kids is five years old and she will be six sometime in October. She attends a school, a multi-racial crèche, and on a few occasions she has asked me and her mother whether we like whites. She has not been able to explain or elaborate on why she would ask such a question. We tell her that we like whites, and we don't have anything against whites.

"Maybe at some stage she will explain to us why she is asking that question, and then we'll be able to deal with that. Maybe it is because of something she heard from other children or adults. But we always tell our children that whether we are white or black, we are just human beings. We should therefore treat each other with respect."

Vincent Barnes

"It is difficult to explain apartheid to the youth. They cannot understand what we went through.

"We had a celebrity match and laid a pitch on Robben Island. Just being there and touring the Island touched me. There were a couple of players who could not believe what they had experienced. Up until today they still cannot believe what people have endured.

"When I talk to my daughter about apartheid or separate development, she finds it very difficult to understand that it happened to people, that people were subjected to inequality.

"Education plays a major role, so our schools must play a part in teaching these values. Whenever I coached a youth cricket team, I would always sit them down and make sure that they knew where they came from, black and white. They should not only associate players like Hansie Cronje with cricket in South Africa – there were older players on the black side who were also good. The white players identify with their icons, but we don't do enough of that. I used to sit down with the youth and many of them were not interested. But some of them wanted to know about the good black players. It is difficult to speak to the youth."

Vincent felt it was possible to teach young people anti-racist values. "Young people are different. It is a lot easier for them to understand, but many of them are naive. Sometime in the mornings I watch the youngsters walking to school and it is black, white, coloured, just walking together and having a chat and laughing. It is all so innocent.

"But when you start talking about racism to a young person like my daughter, they don't understand. My daughter is in the States at the moment. She is 13 years old. When she sends me photos there are Spanish, Mexicans and Cubans all in a class and they are all different. She speaks Spanish and life just goes on. It is just so innocent.

"For some of the older players in our teams, those in their late twenties, it is probably a lot more difficult to grasp. They have to live with each other and a lot of them have accepted different cultures and respect them. That's happened over the last couple of years. I have seen how a young black player has become the best friend of one of the older white players in the team. It is amazing to see the relationship they have. They are always having a go at each other, but they have a wonderful relationship.

"They have respect for each other's cricketing ability and respect for each other's culture and where they come from. It has taken a long time for that to happen."

Rhoda Kadalie

"One should inform children that there was once a government that governed on the basis of having favourites. They preferred green-eyed people to black-eyed people. If you are a government that favours green-eyed people, how are you going to organise your parliament?

"The children will quickly begin to understand what discrimination means, because that is how they discriminate among themselves. They discriminate on the basis of straight hair and *kroes* [curly] hair, fair skin and dark skin, privilege and poverty, cool clothes, poor clothes. They are intelligent enough.

"I tell my daughter about apartheid and she can't believe that some people had to go through the back door, or had to go through a different entrance in the Post Office and so on. Soon those things will be alien to our children. They need to know that there was a system that did that. Then you need to say: 'In order for us to prevent that from happening again, what would you recommend we should do?'

"You need to ensure within the constitutional, democratic, governmental system that any form of racial discrimination will never be tolerated again. You need to educate children about it. You need to take the experiences that they are familiar with and bring that home to them.

"Sometimes my daughter feels it is important to assert that she comes from a black family. One day we had all these kids at our house, and Julia said to them that we are a black family. These white kids asked her why she kept on saying we were a black family and Julia said 'because we are'. It didn't even occur to those kids that we were black, because they don't relate to each other in terms of race. The white boys said: 'To us, Julia is just exotic.' They all want to date her. It is not about race any more. If I talk about us as a black family, I think we are making a point that we don't have to make any more. Race is no longer the determining factor of who we are. We are now South Africans: we love jazz, we love ballet, we love classical music, and that's us."

Rhoda agreed that it was possible to teach young people anti-racist values. "My big gripe is that the Department of Education required schools to do anti-racism workshops, but it backfired horribly, because people were not trained to do this. It is like sexual harassment. Everybody knows it is a problem, but they don't know how to train teachers and learners around the issue of sexual harassment.

"My daughter goes to St Cyprians, a white school where the black kids and the white kids get on very well. On weekends they go to parties together. The school embarked on anti-racism workshops and my daughter came home and she said that she hated these workshops. White kids would try to outdo black kids on non-racialism, and it was very plastic because they still used racist language. Julia said that after the anti-racism workshop, the black girls suddenly called each other 'sister'. Julia did not belong to that because she is now neither white nor black enough. The white kids bent over backwards and patronised. She said that, once again, she felt very alienated.

"When you have an anti-racism workshop, you get the kids to talk about themselves. Some of those kids weren't even aware of racial things and start creating stories. Julia said that many of the stories were blatantly untrue. The way you should deal with anti-racism workshops is to give history lessons and get the kids to research what separate amenities meant for black South Africans. Then the white kids will say, 'Did that really happen to people?' and so on.

"That's how you educate kids around racism. They are young, and it is not part of their history. Many kids don't even know that apartheid existed."

Khusta and Karen Jack

Asked how one explained apartheid to our youth, Khusta Jack said his children, aged five and eight, understood apartheid in terms of the "bad guys" who did bad things to black people. "They understand that the bad guys built an ugly house for Makhulu [their grandmother]. They also understand that the bad guys did not want to allow me to go to a good school."

Karen Jack said that when they visited Khusta's mother in the township, it was easy to explain apartheid to their children. "They can see the whole economic situation and they can understand it. When they go to visit my mother, they ask things like 'Where does Makhulu bath?' and 'Where is the toilet?' They are observers. Now they are bigger, they are beginning to understand, but when they were smaller, they got very worried whenever we left her house and went home.

"They would ask me, 'Why is Makhulu's house so ugly?' Before I could answer, Themba would say it was because Mandela did not like Makhulu. But Mandela liked us because he gave us a nice house. Whenever we visit my mother, the debate is always about housing, and the children pick up these things."

Karen felt that the history books at school should reflect the new version of history. "Apartheid should be easy to explain to the children, but it has to be done in a constructive way, because they are not going to just pick it up along the way."

Both Khusta and Karen thought it was possible to teach young people anti-racist values. "When you tell them that the dog is running after the black guy, they will ask you why. They have very strong values," said Khusta.

"I think the teachers play a big role in this. They are different from us. They have become colour-blind and that is good."

Athena and Manny Sotomi

Manny Sotomi proposed that young people could teach older people anti-racist values. "My son goes to a school with a lot of different races. He only recently realised that he was of a different ilk, and there was no problem, but I think problems will emerge in due course, the older he gets. So it is important to teach young people and instill in them non-racial values."

Athena interjected: "These should not necessarily be non-racial values. I think they just need a value system."

Manny continued: "I am not at all religious, but there is one thing I admire in Christianity or even Islam, and that is their value systems. Whatever your faith, most religions teach you a value system that puts you in good stead. 'Though shall not kill' and things like that – these are the basic rules of humanity. My culture, which is the Yoba of Nigeria, teaches you just to treat people like people. I hope my son is learning that."

"I think he is learning that," Athena remarked. "When he describes things or friends at school, I listen very carefully. With us, with older people, you will say the person was white or black. You will get that description whether you asked for it or not. But he doesn't describe people in that way at all. He will say the person was fat or thin, the person was rude or the person was nice. But he will never say that the person was black or white. That gives you a sense of hope."

Naledi Pandor

"Through the process of freedom, we have created conditions where the majority will govern the country. What I believe we need to put in place are conditions that ensure that whoever governs, does so on the basis of good principles – universal principles of democracy, freedom, non-racialism and non-sexism.

"We need to promote these values through education in all the fields of discipline in our country. If we don't, then we will have problems later. Then we will have poor governors, a lack of accountability, a lack of transparency, and so on.

"Our young black people, coloured and Africans, are going to rule in the future. If they don't understand that when they govern they must promote freedom and democracy, then we are going to have a real problem.

"The ANC has a long history of being concerned about freedom and democracy, from its formation in 1912. If we refuse to infuse those kinds of principles into our youth, by the time they come to rule they will be ruling for themselves and for acquisition. That is when you will have the potential of corruption.

"The media has a job to enhance knowledge of transparency and appreciation for freedom and democracy. They also need to promote institutions of government as institutions that protect and preserve freedom of democracy. We do not give enough scope to Parliament as a promoter of democracy. We need to do much more of that.

"We can teach young people anti-racist values through a range of devices. The curriculum is one, and sport is another. In terms of recreational activity, our children are doing it already, without any enforcement from us. What we need to do now, if one is looking at the school setup, is to do a bit more on diversity education. The [One City Many Cultures] project that you began at the *Cape Times* is an important initiative, but I think it would help if we saw more of that in schools.

"Our children are relating very well as individuals, but I am not sure if they understand the diversity in the community. Our society is very diverse and if they get on well at school, it does not mean that they understand the Muslim community, for instance, or acknowledge other larger cultural differences."

Wilmot James

Wilmot James said that we should explain apartheid to our youth by teaching it properly in schools as part of the curriculum. "Professor Kader Asmal [the Education Minister at the time of this interview] is persuaded by the importance of teaching apartheid and its consequences to our children in school, and I have been commissioned by him to produce a textbook on our history for 2004. I know the Wits History Workshop is focusing this year on the topic, and there are plans with the South African History Project led by Dr June Bam to pursue some of the relevant themes at a forthcoming conference as well. So there is a lot of activity to ensure that teachers teach school children our contemporary history."

Wilmot said it was possible to teach young people anti-racist values. "The question is how one teaches them and what works. A lot of the anti-racism education does not work because it goes into the one ear and out of the other. The best way to teach anti-racist values is to teach children well at school and at home, to teach them modern biology and evolution, but on a very deep, substantive basis.

"Our children should also learn that there should be a single etiquette towards all human beings, regardless of race. The strategy of the teaching is very important and one must understand how children learn anti-racist values before one launches a campaign to do it."

Kenny and Sielie Nolan

Sielie Nolan said that her daughter, who was in matric at the time of the interview, understood what racism meant and was not a racist. "They have African children at their schools and we have spoken to her about racism since she was small."

Sielie explained to her daughter that apartheid was about suffering. "They let you feel low, because only the white man was allowed to be on top. They got all the fancy jobs while we had to do all the dirty work.

"Now we can tell our youth that the government will help them with getting an education so that they can also reach the top. We can now also say that education is important. In the old days education

225

was not important, it was only important for the white man. We were forced to leave school early so that we could go work and earn some money."

Added Kenny: "Now we can encourage our children to continue with their school work. There are many opportunities that we never had."

Asked how we could ensure that apartheid would not happen again, Sielie said: "We must just get racism out of our system. We have to try to live together like brother and sister. We must not look down on each other. Racism is not just about money, it is also about having the correct attitude towards other people."

Sielie believed it was possible and necessary to teach young people anti-racist values. "I think it will be good for all of us. Otherwise, how will one learn about different people's cultures and the things that they do? They call us a rainbow nation, but we can truly become a rainbow nation if we learn to understand each other a lot better.

"The way I see African people is that they are lovely. They are so talkative and so helpful. When you go visit them they treat you well. And they don't talk about how much you drink or how much you eat. That is what coloured people do."

"They stand together," said Kenny, "they are not like our people who just break things down instead of building them up."

My thoughts

There are some people who believe it is not difficult to teach our youth about apartheid because its effects can be seen all around us on a daily basis: in the number of unemployed people, in the sprawling corrugated iron townships that refuse to go away. There are others who believe that we should no longer talk about apartheid and instead focus on the future. There is probably merit in both views.

However, I believe that it is difficult to ignore apartheid. We need to talk to our youth about what happened so that they, and their children after them, can make sure that it never happens again.

It is so easy to forget the past; too easy. And remembering can be difficult. But it is important to make sure that the memory of apartheid remains uppermost in our minds. Too many people have sacrificed too much for us to be where we are today. Sometimes we forget that legal and formal apartheid was still around just over ten years ago.

CHAPTER 13
THE FUTURE

The magic of the not-so-new South Africa

When South Africa became a democracy after almost 50 years of apartheid and almost 350 years of all kinds of oppression of the black majority, it was seen as a miracle in some parts of the world.

What probably remained unsaid or unasked at the time was whether South Africa's new rulers had the ability to proceed from that political miracle and make a success of the country, not only in political terms, but also in economic terms.

There were many white people who expressed their reservations with the new dispensation by stocking up on candles, canned food, guns and ammunition on the eve of the country's first democratic elections on 27 April 1994. There was also a late push by some white right-wing groups to make the country ungovernable on the eve of these elections.

Ten years later, the white right-wing has been effectively neutralised and remains but a shadow of its former self. Many of the white people who had stocked up before the 1994 elections will now not admit to having done so. In the same way, as I mentioned in the introduction to this book, it is difficult to find any white person in South Africa today who will admit that they voted for the National Party during the days of apartheid.

Much has been written about the "M" factor in South African politics, and while the role played by Nelson Mandela cannot be overvalued or overstated, it is important to realise that Mandela was but one of the leaders of the ruling African National Congress who played a role in the transition, albeit a bigger role than most.

Mandela's role was all about reconciliation and nation-building. It was about making sure that the country did not lose crucial white skills at a time when it could ill afford to do so. The people who are now in government, under the presidency of Thabo Mbeki, have to look beyond reconciliation and nation-building and start delivering to a people who have been oppressed for many years and are waiting desperately for the fruits of freedom.

Today's government has had over ten years of experience, and white skills are no longer crucial to South Africa. There are now any number of black people who are more than qualified to run the country and its major industries. However, this does not mean that white people are surplus to requirements in South Africa or are being excluded from the mainstream of society. On the contrary, most of the economic power remains in white hands.

In general, though, South Africa is performing better than most people expected. The economy is performing well, we have a vigilant civil society and we have a Constitutional Court that is not afraid to overrule government if it has to. South Africa has one of the most progressive constitutions in the world.

There are many indications that South Africa is on the right track. However, the country still faces some serious challenges.

I asked the people I interviewed whether they were optimistic or pessimistic about the future of South Africa and if they could change one thing about our country, what it would be.

Vincent Barnes

Speaking about the "new" South Africa, Vincent stated: "I did not expect people to change overnight. In 1995 we won the Rugby World Cup. We were playing a football match in Mitchells Plain at that time and there was this huge screen, the cars were hooting and we could not see what was going on. I couldn't understand what was happening. Somebody just said the Springboks had won and that evening it was chaos. Everybody just embraced the fact and everybody believed that South Africa was united. But a week later, it went to pieces again.

"My expectations were never high. I always felt that it was going to be problematic for all of us for many, many years. I always felt it was going to be very difficult. I wanted to test this unity. I walked gingerly. I wasn't going to go in there and just embrace everybody. I would just sit back and see what was going to happen.

"All of a sudden we had to accept people who had sold us out, who had played on the other side for most of their lives. For ten years, I ostracised these people and saw them as 'honorary white'.

"All of a sudden, we had to accept them. I just could not do it. It took me a long time to forgive and there are still some of them I haven't forgiven. It took me a long time and up to today I remain optimistic, but I knew there were going to be a hell of a lot of problems. I foresaw the problem that we had in cricket. We just rushed in without really thinking about what we were doing."

Vincent said that the one thing he'd like to change was people's mindsets. "I wish I could change people's minds. The way I have been speaking is my perception of the way people generally think. I am not talking of white people only. I am not saying that the coloureds are innocent, because they are in fact the most racist. They won't go to a white person's party and will ask why they were invited to that party.

"If I could make a contribution I would like to change the mindset of people to start believing that no one is superior. No one has the divine right to claim he is superior over the next person, and no one should feel inferior."

Carel Boshoff

I asked Carel whether he was optimistic or pessimistic about the future of our country. "The future calls on one to be positive. A person cannot afford not to find anything positive about their own future. How else can one live?" he asked.

"As for myself, I have enough reason to remain here in South Africa. In fact, I am experiencing this period as a very creative and exciting time. This is not to say that I am part of the new order that is coming into being in South Africa, but because of it, new challenges and questions are placed in front of me.

"I am an Afrikaner and I have to redefine myself. I can give up this identity, or, and this is what makes it attractive and a challenge, I can try to reinterpret it in a creative way.

"I am not a 'happy optimist', an 'everything-is-going-to-be-alright person', a 'win-win person'. But at the same time, it is when people are challenged that the best of human nature comes out. It is exciting in that the challenges we face form part of the greater world out there.

"As an Afrikaner, I ask myself questions about universal humanity. What is it to be a human being if it is not to be from a particular place, time and circumstance? How can I make a contribution, given that one has on the one side a national state, and on the other side a kind of homogenous globalisation? How can I develop a relationship with these two realities that does not consume my individuality?

"I don't know if the views I have just expressed make me optimistic, but they definitively make me active. And if a person is busy doing things, then you have to be optimistic, because you have to believe that what you are doing will work. And there are a lot of things in South Africa that can work."

Khusta and Karen Jack
"The political activists of the seventies and the eighties have to take some blame for things that have gone wrong. We have to point fingers at ourselves, because we slotted into the system very easily, even though we knew it was wrong," said Khusta. "This system offered obscene economic positions or what I call 'conspicuous consumption', where you found many of us living a life of opulence.

"The resentment of the gap that we have created between ourselves and the ordinary people nullifies anything that we do. Our people are looking at their friends who have moved up to this new [economic] level and this creates resentment. As a result, everybody in South Africa is unhappy with what they have. This is because of that distorted economic jump that benefited mainly activists of the seventies and eighties. It is regrettable that we have this kind of situation.

"Other than that, South Africa is a country that is run properly, as far as I am concerned. There are many good things happening. You just need to open your eyes and look around the country on a daily basis and you will find the Western Cape is intact, and you will find that Gauteng is intact. Everything is running smoothly. Occasionally, you will find places which have deteriorated, especially the homelands. But other places have improved."

Karen Jack said that Khusta's mother appreciated the freedom of the "new" South Africa. "Her pension has gone up, she now has running water, she has a telephone, she has electricity and she has a house of her own. I think economically she is alright."

Khusta said that one could not tell his mother, who was 80 years old, anything bad about the ANC government. "She will tell you that she has problems, of course, because her pension is not enough that she can afford a house like ours. Obviously, she is unhappy with that. But she will not believe it if you tell her anything bad about the government. There are many people in a similar economic situation who feel the same."

Asked if they could change one thing about South Africa today, Karen answered, "The position of the Health Department on HIV/Aids."

Khusta felt it was regrettable that in South Africa there was no credible opposition from the same background of struggle as the ANC. This, he believed, would have helped to balance the ANC on certain issues. "I would have preferred it if it was the PAC or Azapo [Azanian People's Organisation] rather than the DA [Democratic Alliance]. The DA is just the mouthpiece of Sandton [an upmarket area in Johannesburg]. Sandton is just a small portion of South Africa.

"We need to correct certain things in South Africa and move towards normalising things, getting what we fought for. However, I don't think we can achieve all of that if we are going to depend on the DA. The DA is honestly stuck in the past, because it wants to protect old privileges."

Karen agreed that a strong opposition would be healthy. "But I also think we need a concerted drive in the areas of black economic empowerment and health. It would help enormously."

Wilmot James
Asked whether the "new" South Africa had lived up to his expectations, Wilmot James answered "yes and no".

"I am pleasantly surprised by our level of political stability and the somewhat clumsy but nevertheless unified way we are moving in the same direction. The vibrancy of our democracy has lost some of its gloss. The quality of our public discourse and the depth of our media instruments, including newspapers, have been very disappointing, and the role of intellectuals has not been up to scratch. It leaves a great deal to be desired," he said.

"The Western Cape has had very poor leadership. The economy has not done much for employment. South Africa, though, is a pleasant place in which to live and we are beginning to learn how to relax with ourselves."

I asked him whether he was optimistic or pessimistic about the future of our country. "I am an optimistic realist. We have, as a people, great talent and many opportunities. Life does depend on what you make of it, so let us get on and make something of South Africa."

And if he could change one thing about South Africa today, what would that be? "I would get South African drivers to drive properly, with legality and etiquette."

Rhoda Kadalie
For Rhoda Kadalie, post-apartheid South Africa had been a big disappointment.

She cited as an example an event in which she was asked to participate by the American Consulate in Cape Town. Also participating were an African-American journalist, who had just written a book about African-American politics; Vincent Saldanha, who worked for the Legal Resources Centre in Cape Town, and Siraj Desai, a Cape High Court judge, who used to be an ANC activist.

"The American journalist presented an interesting political landscape of racial politics in America during and after the civil rights war. He spoke about what drives black Americans politically today, and he mentioned xenophobia. I found it very interesting that the Asians and Hispanics are doing much better than the black community in America and African-Americans have a deep resentment towards the Taiwanese and Japanese.

"After he spoke, Siraj Desai got up and thanked the American journalist for his book, and said how much South Africans admire Martin Luther King and how he was a role model to South African blacks. Vincent then got up and concurred with Siraj. He said he found the history very important, but wanted to ask how September 11 had bedevilled race politics in America. Neither Vincent nor Siraj made any linkage between what the American journalist had said and what was going on in South Africa.

"When I spoke, I said that I could relate to many things the journalist had said in terms of race politics in South Africa. For instance, race politics before 1994 were different to race politics in the liberation era. Before 1994, the rallying cry was non-racialism, so that we almost negated our ethnic identity. After 1995, the political landscape changed and it is interesting to look at racial politics today.

"In a country where you have an African Nationalist government, where you have coloured and Indian people who are told they are equal but in the job market they are not equal, many people are now reassessing their identities to assert who they are in a country where they feel negated once again. I said that the poor implementation of affirmative action was creating a racial resentment in the country and it had led to affirmative inaction in many ways.

"Siraj then got up and said that he wanted to dissociate himself from me. He said he was a very happy citizen and could certainly not detect any of the tendencies that I was talking about. Vincent then got up and said that he found it amazing that Rhoda Kadalie, who comes from a very privileged, middle-class background, could spread this kind of information and he also wanted to dissociate himself.

"They personalised the issue, which made me mad. I said that I found it strange that my colleagues could dissociate themselves from me, when I had empirically verifiable evidence and could prove what I had said.

"I said that this is what bedevilled the discussion around racism. You find many of the old comrades who will talk about racial politics behind closed doors and in public will say something else. There is no solution. There is hope, but there is no solution.

"We have to be prepared to discuss race and racism with our African comrades in the same way that we are prepared to discuss race and racism with whites, coloureds and Indians."

I asked her whether she was optimistic or pessimistic about the future of our country. "The Treatment Action Campaign as a demonstration of vibrant civil society gives me hope, because I think there is a legacy of vibrancy of hope which, when push comes to shove, will be mobilised for the greater good. What also gives me hope is the capacity of people to fight for what is right. Civil society is my only hope."

Rhoda said she was pessimistic about Parliament. "Parliament under the leadership of the ruling party has become an empty shell. Question time has been reduced substantially. The President comes three times a year. Portfolio Committees are not working and the ANC simply uses their majority vote to overrule anything.

"So any bill can be passed. Majority government is not good for democracy and I am hoping for the formation of an opposition in this country.

"The Aids debacle has indicated that even though you have a powerful core of women in senior government positions, they will still toe the party line in order to position themselves. I am very pessimistic about Parliament.

"The other thing I am very sad about is the failure to mobilise loyal opposition in this country. The opposition is always racialised; it is always ridiculed and not respected. The President has never met with the official opposition, which every president has done in every other country.

"I am also worried that all the Chapter 9 institutions which must protect democracy have been co-opted by the government. They are weak. The Gender Commission is hopeless, the Human Rights

Commission is hopeless, and the Public Protector is co-opted. I have no faith in any of those organisations.

"The last thing is the media. The government hates the media and I will fight to death for the right of an independent critical media to exist. Media is always the first casualty when you have a fascist government. You see it in Zimbabwe, where they still introduce laws to curb the media. The way we supported Zimbabwe very clearly indicates to me that your antennae should be out. I am very worried about that under the present government.

"Unless the ANC splits down the middle, I find their notion of the sanctity of the whole versus the individual worrying. Even Mandela will subject himself to the whole. The ANC believes it must keep the party together at all costs, which I find extremely worrying.

"I have studied post-independent countries and democracy in Africa and they all go the same route. They all start in the way that we are going. We have to watch those signals very clearly. Cosatu [Congress of South African Trade Unions] and the SACP [South African Communist Party] are not going to split from the ANC for the next 20 years. And it took 20 years for Zimbabwe to go that route. The problem is that in Africa, democracy is undone in between 15 and 20 years.

"The only thing that gives me hope in South Africa is civil society and the media, but even the media I don't trust. I watch the news on SABC3 and it is equivalent to the news in the old South Africa. There is no difference. It is the mouthpiece of the ruling party. It is not a public broadcaster. It is a state broadcaster."

I asked her what one thing she would change about South Africa today. "I would decentralise government. I believe in federalism and decentralised government, because service deliveries must happen again. Local government is weak. My project [the Impumelelo Innovations Award Trust] is about innovative service delivery, but I hardly get applications from local government, which should be my main applicant. They are weak. They don't have capacity and they don't have space. So if I were the president of this country, I would change that.

"Also, I would encourage the journalists and the opposition.

Multi-party democracy and independent media are the recipes for a good democracy."

Kenny and Sielie Nolan

Asked if post-apartheid South Africa lived up to their expectations, Kenny Nolan said: "Yes, definitely. There has been a big change. You can feel the change."

"Especially between the Africans and the white man," said Sielie Nolan. "In the past you had to be afraid to talk to or walk with a white man or woman. But today we are free to do that. It is a nice feeling. You don't have to feel tense any more. In the old days, they would have just picked you up and thrown you into jail."

"Even if you walked around late at night," added Kenny, "you could end up in jail."

Asked if they were optimistic or pessimistic about the future of South Africa, Sielie replied that she felt positive. "I read an article that said the President wanted to do away with poverty. This will be a good thing. If you don't have money, you don't feel so good. But if he does away with poverty, it means that he will create jobs. If there are jobs, it means that people will have money again. We don't want money for nothing. We want to work for our money."

I asked them what one thing they would change if they were president for a day. Sielie replied: "I would like to tell people to put racism to one side so that we can all move forward."

Kenny added: "I would like to create more jobs for our people."

Naledi Pandor

Naledi Pandor believed that the media and Parliament needed to take up issues that enhanced democracy. She quoted as an example the mission statement of a project that she (in her previous capacity as head of the National Council of Provinces and the Speaker of Parliament) had started, which aimed to confront the perceptions that South Africans had of themselves and of other Africans. The project was called the Parliamentary Millennium Project and its theme was "Perceptions of South Africa and Africa".

"We want to place African achievements in front of South Africans and get them to stop conversing about the negative things such as racism, apartheid and cultural identity.

"We must start talking about other aspects of Africa, which are not always at the forefront. We must talk about the perceptions we hold about the continent and about South Africa. We want to see whether engaging on those perspectives begins to change our perceptions and helps us to get to a different reality.

"We have become concerned that we have a very limited focus when we engage with each other. We tend to engage on apartheid, racism and sexism, and when we talk, we think we all mean the same thing. When I talk about racism, I keep on saying that you need to define it. I could have one idea about racism and you could have a completely different idea. Someone else could have their own idea of what it means. We need to get South Africans talking about different perspectives on the continent.

"In order for us to make a shift, we need to begin looking at ourselves in a new way. Until we do that, we don't believe we are ready to reflect on Africa in a way that takes us into that phase of development we all want to see."

Tracy-Lee Rosslind

I asked Tracy-Lee Rosslind whether the "new" South Africa had lived up to her expectations. "To be honest, as far as the youth goes, it has not," she said. "It upsets me terribly that the coloured children have forgotten what we have gone through. It upsets me that the black children have forgotten what we've been through, and that the white people are so sick of hearing about it that they shut it out.

"I love my country and I will never leave it for all the money in the world. My roots are here. I am going overseas next year and there is not even a possibility that I will not come back. I love being able to walk down into town and to see a guy on a bicycle with a radio and a hooter.

"I love to see people smiling at each other, because we are a free country. But I think the youth need to be educated to appreciate our country, and then everything will be worthwhile. All I wanted was freedom and that is what we got."

I asked her whether she was optimistic or pessimistic about the future of our country. "I am optimistic," she answered. "It can only get better. As bad as it was, it can't get any worse than what happened. Every day it is getting better. We need to have patience to see it through."

I asked her what she would change about South Africa today, to which she replied, "I would change the way people see each other, how we judge one another and how we see ourselves."

Keathelia Satto

Keathelia Satto said that post-apartheid South Africa had not lived up to her expectations. "The country is supposed to have a mixture of a whole lot of races and all these different races are supposed to be able to get jobs and things like that. So far, it seems that the whites still have all the jobs, and now the blacks are also getting the jobs, and the coloureds are still considered a mixed race."

I asked her whether she felt optimistic about the future. "There is hope, but I don't feel good about the future of our country. People elected the President and the President always makes promises, like he says he will give people houses. But he never lives up to what he says. That is why I don't feel good about the future of our country."

I asked her what she would like to change about the country. "I would take away the politics, because politics makes everything corrupt. I would ban politicians."

Melanie Verwoerd

"I always said, at the beginnings of the nineties, that I was sure we were going to make it. I am still sure of that. I am sure that South Africa is going to be a great place and remain a great place. But I have always said it was going to be hard and I still believe that. Maybe even more so than before.

"In a way the new South Africa did not only live up to my expectations, but actually exceeded them. People who visit South Africa talk about the amazing energy in the country. I believe that energy will sustain us in some way. We have to believe, and then things will turn out great. That is the only way we can defeat negativism. We have the potential to be better than great. I almost think we have an obligation towards the rest of the world to make it work. I am very positive that it will work, that despite the difficulties, we will be okay."

Asked what she would like to change about South Africa, Melanie said, "I wish I could change all the socio-economic issues overnight. I would get a grip on the Aids issue, and change the negativity that exists in our country."

Leo de Souza and Obed Zilwa

Both Leo de Souza and Obed Zilwa said they remained positive about the country.

"I love South Africa. I love our people. I love the passion we have. I don't want to live anywhere else," remarked Leo. "South Africa is like any child. It is going to be what we are going to make of it. We have to grow it, we have to nurture it. I am not going to judge South Africa right now, because you can't judge a toddler or a teenager, and that's where we are in our development. We must be realistic in our expectations and we will solve our economic problems and other problems."

Obed echoed Leo's statement: "I love the South African people. I even love Afrikaners. What I love most about them is that their children do not want to be the same as them. They say they don't want to pay for the sins of their fathers. They are prepared to say we must all live together in South Africa."

Obed said he wished that one day his children would be identified as African, in the broader context. "I don't want my children to be identified as coloured, because when you tell people they are coloured, it is like excluding them from our society. I also wish that coloured people would one day stand up and say, 'Ek is nie 'n kleurling nie. Ek is 'n Suid Afrikaner [I am not a coloured. I am a South African].'"

Leo wished that all South Africans could experience the kind of freedom that she experienced. "When you have that, you can solve so many problems. It is just about opening up your mind. My mother found it, I found it, and many other people I know found it. I wish more people could have it."

Trevor Oosterwyk

Trevor was one of the first people I interviewed in 2002 and, at the time, I had not thought of asking my interviewees about their thoughts on the future. However, I was interested to hear Trevor's opinion, and recently received the following answer from him. I feel there is merit in including his response, because unlike other interviewees, he has had the benefit of a few years' hindsight. I thought this appropriate as the last word from the interviewees.

I asked Trevor whether the not-so-new South Africa had met his expectations. "Asking me this question in 2007 is infinitely different to having asked me a few years back. But, the answer is yes, it certainly is turning out to be the dynamic country that I was always dreaming about," he said.

"It is, however, also clear that the revolutionary expectations that we had during the 1980s were not to come about in the way that we would have hoped. And there are so many disappointments in the way certain ANC leaders are dealing with the challenges of a developing society.

"I have much to be concerned about and while we do not engage each other honestly on the issues of the day, we have to agree: the prevalence of corruption, the high levels of crime and the fact that our nation is being decimated by HIV/Aids are all issues that bedevil the task of building the country so it can be a home for all."

I asked him whether he was optimistic or pessimistic about the country's future.

"I am an optimist and I have great faith that in the long run this is going to be a stable and flourishing democracy. It is, however, not going to be easy and we will make many mistakes, but we have to remember that the normal development of the country and its people was perverted by more than 250 years of white domination and apartheid."

And have things changed much in South Africa?

"I am not inclined to deny, as so many seem to today, that much has changed and the country today is a very different one from just a few years ago. Look to the younger people and how they have almost no knowledge or sense of the old South Africa. They are just free to pursue their lives and build relations as free citizens.

"This we cannot deny, but I am mindful that there is a disjuncture between the expectations of change and the stark reality of what the "new" South Africa has become. But we cannot be ahistorical and not face the truth of the dialectic deeply ingrained in notions of change and transformations."

My thoughts

There are many people around the world who have praised the miracle of South Africa's political settlement. How is it, some people wonder, that South Africa's black people, after having been oppressed for so long, could still decide to live in harmony with the white people who oppressed them?

Yet that is one of the beautiful things about this country: our ability to forgive. This is one of the things that give me and others hope for our country, despite the many problems we still face. And there are many problems.

Nevertheless, most of the people I interviewed were positive about the future of South Africa, and one would probably find the same outcome with a broader, more scientific survey of public opinion. Most of them warned, however, that there were key issues that needed to be resolved for us to make real progress.

I do believe that South Africa has come a long way. However, failure to deal with key issues such as poverty, and our inability to properly address the after-effects of apartheid, could cost us dearly and needs proper attention.

Having said that, and realising that race and racism remain at the root of our problems, I feel confident that we *are* grappling with the various issues facing this country and that we will, eventually, be able to overcome them.

FINAL THOUGHTS

When I sat down to interview Rhoda Kadalie for this book, she said to me: "Ryland, are you prepared for this journey that you have undertaken?"

I thought a lot about that comment as I walked away from each of the interviews feeling increasingly perplexed.

For instance, before the interview with Carel Boshoff, I thought he was a right-wing fanatic for wanting to have his own white homeland in South Africa. After the interview, however, I was left thinking that a lot of what he had said made sense. What he was advocating was not very different to what many people in South Africa were doing already: living in segregated residential areas. The only real difference was that he wanted to do it officially.

I decided that confusion was probably the best state to be in to tackle a book of this nature. Race and racism are not simple issues and there are no ready-made and easy answers. Furthermore, answers that apply in one part of the world might not necessarily translate to others.

I hope that I have been able to inspire readers to question and review their viewpoints on racism, and that we as South Africans will continue to look for answers. And while we are searching for answers, I hope that we will continue to talk about this very important issue.

Permissions

From the introduction, pages 3–4, 189 words:

McCall, Nathan. *Makes We Wanna Holler (A Young Black Man in America)*, Vintage Books, New York: 1994, p 346.

I told Danny I did not have a choice in the matter. "You can sit around and intellectualize about race when you want to, and when you get tired of it you can set it aside and go surfing or hang-gliding and forget about it. But I can't. Race affects every facet of my life, man. I can't get past race because white folks won't let me get past it. They remind me of it everywhere I go. Every time I step into an elevator and a white woman bunches up in the corner like she thinks I wanna rape her, I'm forced to think about it. Every time I walk into the stores, the suspicious looks in white shopkeepers' eyes make me think about it. Every time I walk past whites sitting in their cars, I hear the door locks clicking and I think about it. I can't get away from it, man. I stay so mad all the time because I am forced to spend so much time and energy reacting to race. I hate it. It wearies me. But there is no escape, man. No escape."

From Chapter 12, page 209, 312 words:

Jaffer, Zubeida. *Our Generation*, Kwela Books, South Africa: 2003, pp. 64–65.

Ruschka has become aware that my mind is not with her and is tired of the game I pretend to be playing. She is tugging at me to take her onto the beach so that she can go into the water. She is a child who makes a beeline for the sea whenever we visit. Johnny, all his children and myself had this one thing in common. We all loved the water and took to it like fishes. In the summer months, swimming was our main recreational activity.

We are expecting Archbishop Tutu to arrive to head the protest but he has in the meantime been advised to make a detour to Bloubergstrand, a beach on the West Coast to which protestors are being redirected. Ruschka keeps on tugging and demands why she cannot go into the water.

"Those men with the dogs don't want us to go into the water, Ruschka."

"Why, mummy, why?"

I don't know what to say. I suddenly realise that this child has no idea of race. I have never introduced her to the concept and how do I now explain to her that she cannot go into the water because this is a white beach and that she is not white. I do not want to do it. For so long our central passion has been building a non-racial society where all of us can just be human beings, not punished for the colour of our skin.

She is insisting. What should I say?

I swallow hard. "Well, Ruschka, you can't go into the water because you are not white."

For a moment, she is still, as if pondering what I have said. I am relieved that the tugging has stopped. Then she looks down at her white track-top and grips it with two fingers, pulling it away from her body. "But, mommy, I am white."

Bibliography

ANC website. http://www.anc.org.za/ancdocs/history/mbeki/1996/ sp960508.html ("I am an African" speech by President Thabo Mbeki)

Biko, Stephen Bantu. *I Write What I Like*, The Bowerdean Press, London: 1978.

Frederickson, George M. *Racism: A Short History,* Princeton University Press, Princeton New Jersey: 2002.

Hamilton, Charles V., Huntley, Lynn, Alexander, Neville, Guimaraes, Antonio Sergio Alfredo, and James, Wilmot (ed.), *Beyond Racism: Race and Inequality in Brazil, South Africa, and the United States,* Lynne Reiner Publishers, London: 2001.

Jaffer, Zubeida. *Our Generation*, Kwela Books, South Africa: 2003, pp. 64–65.

King, Martin Luther, Jr. *The Words of Martin Luther King. Selected and with an introduction by Coretta Scott King,* 2nd ed., Newmarket Press, New York: 1984.

McCall, Nathan. *Makes We Wanna Holler (A Young Black Man in America)*, Vintage Books, New York: 1994, p 346.

Steele, Shelby. *The Content of our Character*, Harper Perrennial, New York: 1998.

West, Cornell. *Race Matters*, Vintage Books, New York: 2001.